SPRATTON

A
Village History

Written and compiled by
Enid Jarvis and Michael Heaton

Spratton Local History Society

Spratton – A Village History

ISBN 0-9549857-0-2

First published in 2005 by
Spratton Local History Society
9 Church Road
Spratton
Northampton
NN6 8HR

Local Heritage *initiative*

 Heritage Lottery Fund   Nationwide   The Countryside Agency

Front cover: 1918 Spratton village primary school with schoolmaster Mr Harry Smith. 1896 O S map
Back cover: A view of Spratton from the Brixworth Road
Printed and bound by Elpeeko, Outer Circle Road, Lincoln

CONTENTS

Spratton.

Introduction

For a number of years, Spratton Local History Society has been collecting together photographs in order to form a village historical archive. These photos, carefully prepared and stored on computer by the society's archivist Michael Heaton, formed the basis of our research for this book and determined the topics initially covered in each chapter. Inevitably we found that more information was needed and we have tried our best to give a balanced picture of the village.

We are most grateful for the 'Awards For All' lottery grant we received to buy computer equipment to record and store our collection and also for the 'Local Heritage Initiative' grant that has enabled us to produce a beautifully designed book recording the history of Spratton.

Michael Heaton has spent nearly 18 months persuading people in the village to lend us their photos and to tell us all about them and the people and scenes they depict. He has spent many hours carefully preparing the final selection for publication. Enid Jarvis has spent as long poring over books, old documents and tape recordings to produce the text. We are grateful to Lesley Lusher and Clare Lee from Lincolnshire for help with the design and for presenting the results of our labours so attractively.

We should like to thank the many people who have helped us so enthusiastically, turned out the contents of their photo albums and shared their memories with us. We are especially grateful to the late Peter Saul for allowing us to use his extensive collection of historical material. Twenty nine of Peter's photos are displayed in the book. We could not have managed without the cheerful help of Ron Bell. His unfailing memory has checked our facts, added dates and put names to faces in faded photos of long ago. We are extremely grateful to Athene Frisby for the chapter on lacemaking. No other publication as far as we are aware has such a detailed account of the lace industry in Spratton. Athene was able to find photos for us that we had

never seen before and we were delighted when we found samples of Spratton lace in the Northampton Record Office's C A Markham Collection (CAM 890) to add to the chapter. We are grateful to Sue Matthews for her hard work recording the activities of the Merry Comrades in Spratton and to Dick Spearman and Peter Churchill for the articles on football and cricket. We should like to thank the following who have given up their time to write sections of the text: Terry Greenwood, Kathleen Saul, Angus Walker, Adrian Baker and Graham Smith.

We have had a great deal of help with our research. We are grateful to Rosemary McCarlie, our tutor at a series of ten local history evening classes held here in the village, who carried out extensive searches for us in the Northampton Record Office. We should like to thank Colin Haddon of the Northampton and Lamport Railway for providing us with photos and information about Spratton Station and the railway line and also Dr Diane Atkinson of London whose advice and help on William Rhodes Moorhouse VC set us off an many new tracks to explore. We have made much use of the Rev G Raw's Parish Newsletters from 1906-1942 kindly lent to us by Ron Buckby and also the Rev J Llewelyn Roberts' Parish Newsletters from the 1890s provided by Rev B Lee. We are grateful to Michael Benn who constantly provided us with genealogical material from his invaluable datebase and to longstanding village families for their help with 'detective' work on some of the photographs. Mary Spearman and her Canadian relatives have helped with family information and Nancy Branson sent her father's memoirs from the Isle of Wight. Older members of the village have recorded their memories on tape and these have been used in the book. We are grateful to Kathleen Saul, John Tarrant, the late Caroline Green and the late Sidney Holt for giving up their time to speak into our tape recorder. Staff at Northampton Central Library Local Studies Department, Northampton Chronicle and Echo and Northamptonshire Record Office have been most courteous to us and provided documents, books and photographs as well as helpful advice.

We are very grateful to everyone who has helped to provide the wonderful photographs showing Spratton folk and village scenes from 1904 onwards. We should particularly like to thank for loaning us photographs: Kathleen and the late Peter Saul, Frances Roseblade, Rev Canon Brian Lee, Michael Heaton, Enid Jarvis, Mary Spearman, Edward Barrett, Colin Richardson, Gwen Morgan, Sheila Bradshaw, the late Caroline Green, John Wykes, Keith Birch, Tony Griggs, Eileen Costello, Eric Johnson (from Long Buckby), Graham Billingham, George Martin, Graham Smith, Ian Gilby, Joe Kelly, the late Janet McKenzie, Joyce Walton, Jean Sutch, Doris Lloyd Thomas, Marlene Haynes, Michael Benn, Michael Wright, Tom Smith, Ursula Dickens, Natalie Lourie Hartwell (USA), Terry Greenwood, Sue Roberts, Sheila Burgoine, Sarah Bradnam, Sarah Passey, Ray Hammond, Peter Tucker, Peter Churchill, Pauline Bending, Maria Costello, Jeff Tite, Harry Copson, Gerald Laste, G Best, Elaine Armstrong, Devon Malcolm, Ben Cohen, Barry Frenchman and Andrew Elliott. Stuart Hadaway of the RAF Museum in Hendon kindly spent time showing us a replica of the BE2b aeroplane flown by William Rhodes-Moorhouse in 1915 and we are pleased to be able to print a large number of their extensive collection of Moorhouse family photographs with the approval of The W B Rhodes-Moorhouse VC Charitable Trust. Our thanks also to Simmons Aerofilms, Cooper and Newton Museum, Getty Images, Pat Rowley Collection, Tony Heighton, 'Mapped Out', Tim Moolman of Keigs/Island Photographics, and RSM Photographers for the use of their photographs.

Other valuable help has been given by the Northamptonshire Family History Society, the Church of England Primary School Spratton, Spratton Hall School, the Commonwealth War Graves Commission, the late Air Commodore John Jarvis, and the Air Historical Branch of the RAF.

E J
March 2005

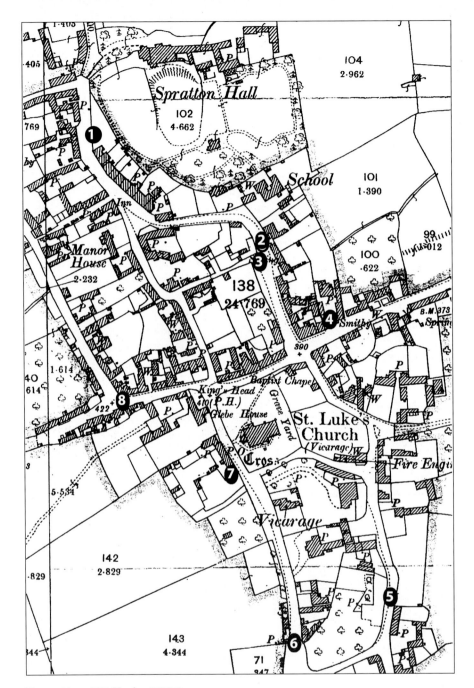

Spratton Wells in 1894

1. Lady Erskin's pump - surprisingly not marked on the OS map.

2. Mains Well near school.

3. Tassell's Well or Treadwell's Well, found to have a pump erected over it.

4. Blacksmith's Well.

5. Bateman's Well.

6. Austin's Well.

7. Presumed to be the location of Manning's or Osbourne's Well, which had to be linked to the private well in Canon Robert's field, but even then does not seem to have been productive, and was probably abandoned soon after 1894.

8. Pound Well - the Pound was on the opposite corner of Backside or High Street.

Chapter One

A HISTORY OF SPRATTON

Site

The village of Spratton stands on a spur of land between 70m and 135m above sea level in the Northampton Uplands, a continuation of the Cotswold Hills. The Uplands are formed of limestone which has been thickly covered with glacial deposits of clay and sand. Where the sub-soil is clay there is good fertile farmland and wooded areas; where there is mainly sand, for example on the highest ground, gorse and broom grew freely in former times. Reminders of this can still be found in the street name 'Gorse Road' and in the name of the house 'Broomhill'.

The village is almost completely surrounded by streams: Stowe Brook flowing into Hollowell Reservoir, Teeton Brook flowing through Ravensthorpe Reservoir, Spratton Brook flowing out of Ravensthorpe Reservoir and Backstone Brook within the parish itself. Despite the fact that there was no mains water supply to Spratton until 1950, there was no lack of water for those who lived here as many houses had private wells or pumps. There were also eight public wells. Some wells can still be found in the village, although none is now used for supplying water.

The sandy nature of the soil has enabled some important discoveries to be made by aerial photography. Prehistoric trackways, enclosures and cropmarks have shown up on sites immediately to the north and west of the village. A large quantity of worked flints (both Neolithic and Bronze Age) has been found as well as fragments of Iron Age pottery. Roman pottery fragments found to the south clearly indicate a small Roman settlement. Small amounts of early Saxon pottery have also been discovered. The heart of the village has always lain some distance from the main Northampton to Leicester road (A5199). A deep hollow-way at the northern end of the village which continued the present High Street northwards, and another at the southern end of Church Road shows that Spratton once lay on a north/south road later replaced by the 18th century turnpike road and the modern A5199. Immediately to the north-east of Spratton Hall, a series of banks and ditches suggests the remains of the former manor house nearby.

Name

The name Spratton was first used in documents in 1613. Before that the settlement was referred to as Sprottun, Sprotton, Sprotone, Spretone and Spretton. The word is thought to come from the Old English *spreot* which means 'a pole' and *tun* meaning 'a farmstead' or 'village'. It is difficult to know precisely what this means but it probably means a farmstead made or enclosed by poles of wood (straight young trees, sprouts or saplings).

Domesday Book 1086

There is an entry for Spretone in the Domesday Book, the great inventory of England made for William the Conqueror to enable him to find out how wealthy his new kingdom was. Three members of the French nobility had been given land in this area: the Count of Mortain, Robert de Bucy and the Countess Judith, a niece of William himself and widow of one of the last Anglo-Saxon Earls. The surveyors of the kingdom found 28 people (and one slave) living in Spretone with six ploughs between them. There were two mills and a valuable six acre meadow as well as approximately 495 acres of land. They noted that the settlement was flourishing again after the troubles of 1066 and the value had doubled. It was now valued at 85s.

The first recorded names of Spratton village people were written down by the surveyors of William I. We know little about them except that they owned and worked on sections of land and their names were William, Osmond, Ralph, Robert, Durand, Wulfmer and Rohais.

Lords of the Manor

From Domesday onwards land in Spratton was owned by a number of families, not just one, and consequently there was more than one 'Lord of the Manor'. The manor at Little Creaton (then part of the parish of Spratton) was held from Norman times by the de Creton family and eventually passed in 1548 to a wealthy yeoman, Thomas Twigden. Thomas's grand-daughter, Amphillis, baptised in Spratton Church in 1602, went on to become the great-great grandmother of George Washington, first president of the United States of America.

The Count of Mortain's lands (1086) passed through various owners until in the 12th and 13th centuries they were in the hands of the Arden family. Sir John Swinford, a follower of John of Gaunt, the Duke of Lancaster, married into this family and became Lord of the Manor through his wife, Joan. He died in 1371 and his elegant, alabaster tomb is one of the prized possessions of Spratton Church. Sir John's daughter, Elizabeth, married Roger Chambers who became Lord of the Manor in his turn and it continued in the Chambers family for many years, often passing through the female line and thus changing names (e.g. Maxe, Inguersby).

The Countess Judith's lands (1086) were eventually sold to Thomas Chambers in 1428 and absorbed into the Chambers / Arden manor.

Another manor, held by the Downhall family of Geddington, was bought in 1547 by Laurence Manley, a wealthy mercer (linendraper) and several times Mayor of Northampton. Laurence Manley had bought the patronage of the church after it had been confiscated by King Henry VIII from the Abbey of St James in Northampton. He had also bought Maxe's manor. By the middle of the 16th century the Manleys, together with the Twigdens, were of major local standing in the area.

Mediaeval Spratton

From the Domesday Book 1086, to 1538 when the first Parish Register of Births, Marriages and Deaths was begun, it is difficult to gain a detailed picture of Spratton since there are few written records. From the wills left by those of some standing in the village, the impression is gained of a religious and godfearing people, dutifully leaving money to the church ('the church of the blessed Andrew the Apostle of Spratton'), but also leaving other items of value such as 'a stryke of barley', 'one stryke of malt' and 'my best sheep'. Ewes and sheep feature largely as items of value as do crops.

1464 Mediaeval brass of Robert Parnell in Spratton Church

1464 Johanna Parnell. The Parnells are probably related to Thomas Parnell, vicar of Spratton 1499–1511 (see pages 33, 35)

The greater part of the land in the village was farmed communally as 'open 'field (see page 10) and many village families held individual shares of land. Roads and bridges were maintained communally and no one landowner or nobleman had charge of affairs as was the case in some nearby villages. The parish economy was based on livestock as well as barley, rye and peas. There was at least one water mill and also a fish farm. Horses were used as draught animals and the many references to sheep in wills suggest some villagers were deriving an income from wool. Looms and equipment for weaving were also passed on in wills.

In the 12th and 13 centuries Northampton was nationally a most important town with great parliaments held there as well as jousting and hunting for the many monarchs who visited. Huge fairs and markets were held regularly. We can assume that some of the people of Spratton, only 8 miles away, visited Northampton and shared in this prosperity. What happened to them when the Black Death struck in 1348-1350 and bubonic plague killed off so many in the whole country? It has been estimated that the population of the county fell by about 40% under the impact of a series of epidemics and again we must assume that Spratton had its share of suffering.

Spratton Church

By far the oldest building in Spratton is the church, probably there in Saxon times but enlarged and strengthened in 1120 in the days of Henry I. This simple Norman church consisted only of a nave, but a bell tower was built in about 1195 and a north aisle added. Parts of the old church still survive. At about this time, the church with one acre of land was given to the important Abbey of St James in Northampton by Simon de Creton. Bequests such as this by the faithful over time increased the wealth of the great monasteries. In 1269 the Archdeacon of

The Norman south door of Spratton Church restored in 1988.

taper to set upon the high altar whenever the priest is at mass'. Thomas Hartwell 1520 asked 'to be buried in the church of Sprotton under the lamp' and Margaret Parker 1542 left 'to the church a wax torch'.

In 1505 John Chambers, a later lord of the manor and a descendant of Sir John Swinford, built a chantry chapel on the north side of the chancel (now the vestry holding the organ) and in his will he left land and money to pay for a priest to pray for his soul and the souls of his parents, his brother William and his wife Elizabeth.

Northampton was appointed to the church at Spratton and the lands given to the Abbey included Broomhillwell. Our first recorded vicar was Henry de Briggestok who was inducted on 29th December 1274.

In the 14th century the community of Spratton was obviously still flourishing and much rebuilding and extension to the church was carried out. The south aisle was added, the churchyard cross erected and a splendid new chancel built around the old Norman one. From this period dates the tomb of Sir John Swinford (died 1371) in place of honour by the altar and it is tempting to think that he, as lord of the manor, had a hand in this expression of religious faith by organising or paying for the new building work. A second tomb stands by the altar with no discernable marks to tell us who was buried there. Earlier historians suggested it was the tomb of Sir John's wife, Lady Joan.

It is difficult to imagine from looking at the church today what it would have looked like before the Reformation. Little has survived of the colour and exuberance of mediaeval times in the form of wall paintings or stained glass. We know that Sir John Swinford's tomb was brightly painted because minute fragments of the paint remain but of the altar, lamps and images we can only turn to the wills of the residents of Spratton of the time to get an idea. Devout villagers left money, sheep, barley or malt to buy wax to keep the many candles alight. There would seem to have been lights in Spratton church for St Andrew, St Barnabas and St Nicholas as well as a sacrament light, a rood light and a sepulchre light which at Easter burned continuously from Good Friday to Easter Sunday. Thomas Heywood 1551 bequeathed 'the price of a taper of wax to buy one

All this was soon to change when Henry VIII began his attack on the Catholic Church with the Act of Supremacy in 1534. His commissioners came to Northamptonshire and within five years all the monasteries had been closed down and their lands sold. The people petitioned the king to spare the Abbey of St James which had been good to the poor but no exceptions were made. In Edward VI's reign the mediaeval altars in the parish churches were removed together with the lights, images, and screens. Any wall paintings were white-washed over. Is this perhaps when the head of the cross in Spratton churchyard was removed and smashed? The chantry chapel was suppressed and the money left by John Chambers to employ a priest was seized. In 1552 all the vestments, sacred vessels and ornaments of parish churches were confiscated.

Generally there was not much resistance to these massive changes in Northamptonshire. Nor did many people object when Queen Mary came to the throne in 1553 and restored Catholicism. After five years, however, Mary was dead and Elizabeth (1558) followed her father and moved away from Roman Catholicism. In Spratton the vicars Hugh Witter, William Manley and Robert Clarke guided their flock through these troubled times. If they spoke out, they do not seem to have lost their positions. However, it is interesting to look at the burials recorded in the village for the decade of the 1550s. Ninety three folk died and were buried as against 59 the previous decade and 32 in the following one. In 1558, the year that Elizabeth came to the throne, 17 people died, 12 of them adult males aged between 22 and 45 years. Ten of these men died in the months January to November leading up to Elizabeth's accession and the remaining two died on the same day two weeks later.

None is known to have made a will. It is not too fanciful to suspect that some of these Spratton men spoke out about the changes being imposed upon them and died violently disagreeing with their neighbours as a result.

Plague in the 16th and 17th centuries

Spratton was no rural backwater, cut off from the rest of the country. It lies only 8 miles from Northampton on the old mediaeval road from London to Leicester. Some of its people probably traded in the markets of Northampton and worked on the big estates nearby. Holdenby House, the largest private palace in England, had been built in 1580 by a favourite of Queen Elizabeth I, Sir Christopher Hatton, and both the queen and her successor James I visited the house with their courts. Charles I was a prisoner there after the Battle of Naseby. It is surprising therefore that the people of Spratton did not seem to suffer greatly in the numerous outbreaks of bubonic plague in 16th and 17th centuries. Figures are given below for burials in Northampton and Spratton in four years when the plague was particularly virulent in England.

Burials in the plague years				
	1578	1603	1605	1638
Northampton	180 (68)	231	625 (139)	565 (122)
Spratton	3 (?)	10 (11)	7 (8)	20 (14)

Shown in brackets is the normal annual burial rate, where known, averaged over 5 years

Spratton would seem to have survived the sickness in 1578 and 1603 and even the terrible outbreak in 1605, but in 1638 the number of burials increases significantly.

The English Civil War

The town of Northampton declared for Parliament in 1642, repaired its walls and became the strongest garrison in the south midlands. Its traders did good business selling boots and horses to Cromwell's army. The gentry of the county declared their allegiances too, with the Earl of Northampton and Baron Spencer siding with the king together with the wealthy Wakes, Isham, Vaux and Brudenell families. For Parliament were the Cartwrights, Claypoles, Drydens, Knightleys and Thorntons.

With the main London/Leicester road passing so close it is highly likely that the residents of Spratton experienced the general fear and excitement. In October 1643 a royalist raiding party on its way to attack Northampton passed through Long Buckby, Holdenby and Chapel Brampton seizing horses everywhere they could along the route. In June 1645, King Charles I arrived in Market Harborough, while Cromwell's army under General Thomas Fairfax marched from Banbury to meet him and spent the night of June 13th quartered at Guilsborough. Oliver Cromwell joined them and a council of war was held. Possibly some soldiers were billeted that night in nearby Spratton. And were horses from the village commandeered for the next day's march to Naseby where the most decisive battle of the Civil War was fought? Two huge armies on the move in the close vicinity must have had some effect on the generally peaceful life of the villagers. By February 1646 King Charles I was a prisoner in Holdenby House before being taken to London for his trial and execution.

Under the commonwealth formed by Oliver Cromwell a Presbyterian regime was set up in the Church of England and 96 parish priests in Northamptonshire were ejected and replaced by Presbyterian ministers. Any clergyman using the Book of Common Prayer in church faced the risk of banishment. Statues and crucifixes were destroyed. The arms of our 14th century churchyard cross may well have been torn down during this period, rather than in Tudor times. In Spratton, the Rev John Ward MA seems to have survived these troubled times. He became vicar in November 1626 and remained in his post for 34 years until he died in April 1660, the year that Charles II was restored to the throne. He was buried in the church, although no memorial to him now remains.

Farming

Up to the 18th century farming in Spratton was open-field. There were five very large open fields round the village named Woodfield (to the east and north-east), Bridge Field (to the south), Middle Field (to the south-east), North Ryefield (to the north-west) and South Ryefield (to the south-west) and these were divided into long, narrow strips of land. The strips were individually owned but generally communal grazing was allowed all over the land after harvest. Aerial photography has revealed the ridge and furrow marks of these common fields still visible round most of the village. Grass boundaries separated the strips and farmers worked together, making group decisions to ensure the fertility of the land. Individual farmers were fined if they broke the bye-laws agreed in the manorial courts. In 1564 one of the orders issued was, *it is decreed that the field shall not be broken up until the most part of the whole town is agreed...upon pain of every man that does to the contrary 10 shillings*

Another order stated,

it is decreed that no occupier shall keep above two old geese and a gander upon pain of every old goose so kept to the contrary 40 pence and for every time that any of their geese shall be taken in the cornfield 4 pence

The Brixworth orders of 1592 stated,

It is decreed that no person shall keep their sheep upon any land sown with any corn or grain upon pain of 14 pence for every default

Enclosure

Custom and tradition played a large part in the open field method of farming but it was wasteful of time and energy as farmers moved around their strips, often scattered about the fields. New developments were slow in coming as group decisions had to be made. With the steady rise in population in the 18th century there was an increasing demand for food and improvements in farming methods were needed. Some of the first lands to be enclosed in England were in Northamptonshire and Spratton's Inclosure Award was granted in 1766. The scattered strips of land were re-allocated so that farmers had all their land in one or more manageable units. They could then farm as they wished without the need to co-operate with everyone else. Farmers and large landowners profited as land values rose and they were free to develop their land as they chose. The landscape round the village changed dramatically. In place of the huge open fields, hedges, trees and copses appeared forming boundaries round each farmer's land.

In Spratton 26 families and two charities (the Trustees for the Church and the Poor of Spratton; the Trustees for the Poor Children of Coventry) put forward claims for enclosed land, the largest landowner being Francis Beynon of Spratton Hall with just under 300 acres mainly in Bridge Field and the South Ryefield. Other farmers in the village with over 100 acres at enclosure were Thomas and Millicent Hide; Sir Thomas Ward and his son Richard; Sarah Atkins, a widow; the Rev Christopher Hodgson, the vicar, who received land in lieu of tithes which were being faded out; the family of William Lantsbery who died in 1801 and is buried in the churchyard; Thomas Chapman who died in 1804 and is buried in the churchyard; and Cory Chadwick.

Part of the 1739 printed amendment to the 1721 Act granting permission to charge tolls on the Northampton to Leicester road past Spratton.

Those villagers without land lost a number of their ancient rights such as the right to graze their cow or pig on common land. For those with not even a garden to their cottage, this was serious. However there do not appear to have been riots in Spratton as there were in other villages such as West Haddon and Raunds, and the people found other ways of making a living.

Roads

In the 16th and 17th centuries national roads played an increasingly important part in trade and general movement about the country. The population had increased and there were demands for food and raw materials. Inns became very important for a new class of traveller trading in the major towns – wealthy horse-dealers, wool-staplers, barley-factors and cattle drovers. Highgate House on the London to Leicester

1959 *An atmospheric photograph taken late on a winter's afternoon in 1959 of a 9F Class No 92154 pulling empty coal wagons past the signal box at Spratton. A car waits at the level crossing. There were many such level crossings in Northamptonshire before all the branch lines were closed.*

road became a well-known high class inn and in Spratton The White Horse Inn prospered.

In the 18th century turnpike trusts were set up by Act of Parliament to repair, maintain and improve the most important roads in the country. In 1721 the road out of Northampton to Leicester passing Spratton (the modern A5199) was turnpiked. There were toll gates at Kingsthorpe, Brampton Bridge, Thornby and Welford. Stage coaches carried both the mail and passengers and were soon cutting down the times of long-distance journeys. Companies competed with one another for trade, but most were clear in their advertisements that they would "not be accountable for the loss of any jewels, rings, plate or watches." The danger of being robbed on the public highways was not particularly great in this part of Northamptonshire, but the notorious Dick Turpin occasionally ventured into other parts of the county. The turnpike milestone from Brampton Bridge (showing distances from Brampton to Northampton 3 miles; to Welford 11 miles; to London 69 miles) can now be seen in the Abington Park Museum, Northampton.

Turnpike roads were closed in 1888 when the responsibility for main roads passed to the newly created county councils.

Canals

Northamptonshire did not benefit as much from canals for water transport as had at first seemed possible. The high cost of constructing locks in and out of Northampton meant that the canal was built a few miles to the west of the town. The Grand Junction Canal was opened for traffic in 1799 and enjoyed some 50 years of prosperity, bringing cheaper coal and Welsh slate into the county. Welsh slate can be seen gracing the rooftops of Spratton houses.

The proposed Union Canal from Leicester to Northampton only ever reached Welford and was never a great commercial success. Nevertheless, goods were brought in to Spratton overland from Welford.

Railways

Northampton was also by-passed when the London to Birmingham railway was built in 1838 with Blisworth and Roade being the nearest stations.

On 16th February 1859 a branch line (London and North Western Railway) was opened from Northampton to Market Harborough, stopping at Brampton, Brixworth and Lamport. It was a single line track and two trains each way ran daily. Mr Robert Stephenson, son of the famous George Stephenson and one of the resident engineers, accompanied the first train together with Mr Dunkley, the contractor.

In 1864 after urgent appeals from people in Spratton LNWR opened a new station where the line crossed the Spratton to Brixwworth road, with four trains each way stopping daily. By 1871 the Station Master was Isaac Hicks and in 1874 Abraham Matthews took over the job. Because of increased usage another track was built and the double track line was opened on 4th August 1879.

On 23rd May 1949 Spratton Station was closed to commercial traffic, but the last train ever to run – a 'passenger special' – ran on 15th August 1981.

Work in Spratton

From earliest recorded times we know that those living in Spratton relied heavily on agriculture for their living and their way of life. Mediaeval villagers here grew barley, rye and peas and kept cattle and sheep. They also wove woollen cloth.

Spratton was an 'open' village which meant that anyone could come and live here. Other 'closed' villages in the area were owned by wealthy landowners who controlled all the houses within their parish. When they pulled down cottages, the farm labourers had to find somewhere else to live and Spratton offered affordable accommodation. Cottages here became crowded with the poor of other parishes as well as our own. Sometimes six or seven people of both sexes slept in one room and 'the common decencies of life were impossible.' Spratton had a reputation for immorality and quarrelling by 1861. By this time nearly half the working men in Spratton (46.2%) relied on the land for their livelihood. Some were farmers and graziers but most were labourers either on farms around the village or farms further afield (when they had a long walk at the beginning and the end of the day to and from their place of employment).

Up until about 1820 this had not been the case. In 1777 one third of the workers in Spratton (32.8%) were involved in textiles. They were weavers, flax dressers and wool combers working generally from home. Women were helping to augment the family income by making lace. However, once machinery began to be used for the production of textiles in the West Riding of Yorkshire worsted weaving as a cottage industry declined and in Northamptonshire it collapsed almost overnight. By 1841 only 4.8% of men in Spratton were working in textiles and by 1881 it had fallen to 0.9%. Men without employment desperately sought other work as agricultural labourers and women took on jobs as domestic servants. Others learned the craft of shoemaking and together with their families became outworkers for shoe firms in Northampton. Shoemaking in Spratton grew slowly, however, and at its peak did not employ more than 12.7% of the working men in the village. In 1873 ironstone quarries were opened between

The main occupations of wage earners in Spratton 1771 – 1901

Occupation	1777 %	1841 %	1881 %	1901 %
Agriculture	20.8	46.2	37.8	23.5
Textiles	32.8	4.8	0.9	0.6
Shoemaking	3	8	8.4	12.7
Domestic Servants	8.9	16.2	20.3	28.7
Craftsmen	11.9	10	11.6	6
Shopkeepers	10.4	7.7	8.4	13.6
General Labourers	8.9	2.4	11.3	10.7
Professional	3	4.4	2.5	4

Paupers and those living on independent means have not been included. The figures for 1777 are taken from the list of men aged 18 years to 45 years available for military service, and so do not include women's occupations. The figures for 1841, 1881 and 1901 are taken from the census returns, when women's occupations were recorded in greater detail.

Mid 19th century *With the collapse of the textile industry some workers in Spratton became boot and shoemakers. They worked in their own homes with materials supplied by firms in Northampton.*

1930s *Samuel Blundell, one of Spratton's blacksmiths*

Brixworth and Spratton and a number of Spratton men found employment as labourers.

It was not until the second half of the 19th century that women's occupations began to be recorded on the census returns in any numbers. In Spratton they flocked into domestic service, sometimes setting up on their own as laundresses, dressmakers, charwomen and shop keepers. A number of widows in Spratton took over the running of their late husband's shops or public houses.

By 1901 twelve families in Spratton employed domestic servants. Some had just one young 15 or 16 year old girl from the village as a general servant. Richard Gilby, a farmer, and his family, for example, employed 15 year old Alice Higgs, and Henry Surridge, the master sweep, employed Maria Buckby aged 15 years. Other families employed 'professional' servants who came from outside the village and took on specific roles in the household. The two Miss Bevans at Spratton House, the five Miss Featherstones at Cotfield, Lord and Lady Erskine at Spratton Hall, Mr and Mrs Edward Moorhouse at Spratton Grange and Mr and Mrs Simson at Broomhill all employed large numbers of staff not only to run their houses but to look after the grounds as well. The larger households also employed grooms and coachmen to work in the stables.

The largest establishment in Spratton seems to have been Spratton Grange owned by Mr W H Foster. The tenants in 1901 were the very wealthy Mr and Mrs Moorhouse and their four children (two teenage girls Ann and Mary, a 7 year old boy Edward, and young William away at boarding school at Harrow). They employed a butler and housekeeper to head a below stairs group consisting of footman, lady's maid, cook, housemaid, kitchenmaid and general servant.

The children were cared for by a governess, head nurse, under nurse and nurserymaid. Outside they employed a head gardener, a coachman and two stablehands. The servants in the house came from as far away as Scotland, Devonshire and London while the under nurse was Louise Horst from Switzerland.

The governess to the Moorhouse children at Spratton Grange, Emily Davison, aged 28, was an enthusiastic suffragette. She became well-known when in 1913 she threw herself under the king's horse at the Derby and was killed.

Population of Spratton 1801 – 2003	
Year	**Population**
1801	776
1851	898
1901	773
1951	793
2003	1222

1900 *In the late 19th century there was a rise in demand for domestic servants. Sarah Ellen Webb was lady's maid to Miss Mildred Bevan of Spratton House.*

1965 *An aerial view of Spratton with School Road, Manor Road and the car park of the King's Head public house in the foreground. To the left, Yew Tree Lane winds past Gilby's Farm and the old Rose and Crown, while to the right, off Church Road, the St Luke's Road development can be seen. The field at the top right of the photograph is where the Ryefields houses now stand.*

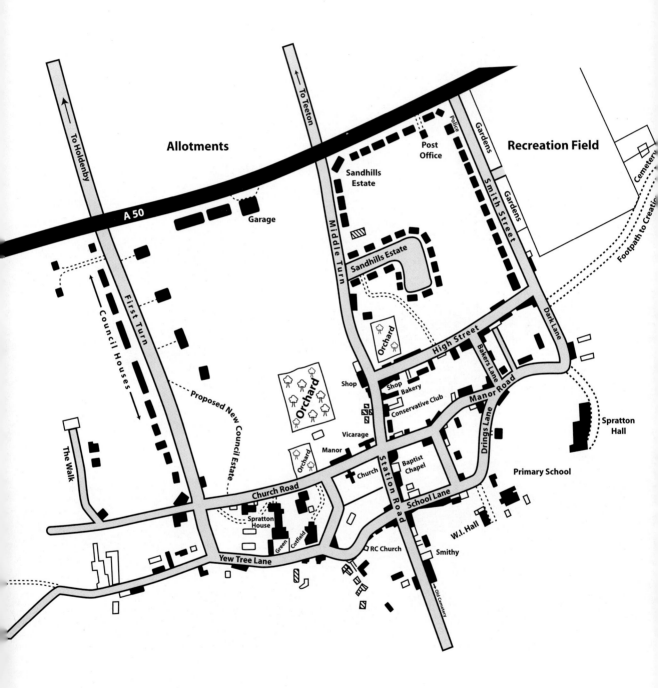

Spratton in the 1950s

Chapter Two

AROUND THE VILLAGE

1930s *Brixworth Road (formerly Station Road)*

A 1930s postcard of the country lane leading out of the village towards Spratton Station (LNWR) and Brixworth. It shows

1 and 2 Johnny Richardson's Family Grocer's store where Ron Bell was employed as a grocer's boy. The shop sold not only groceries, but also hardware and stationery. It was also the Post Office. Before the house became a grocer's shop it was lived in by Charles Tyrrell, a tailor.

3 The Richardson's warehouse.

4 and 5 Thatched cottages lived in by Percy Richardson, Johnny's son, and Bob Balderson.

6 The smithy. Samuel Blundell was the blacksmith followed by Jack Bowers.

7 Mr and Mrs Bard Leeson's house.

8 Charles Court's house.

9 Mr Bates' house.

10 A Washhouse.

A 1950s *postcard showing the grocer's shop when it was owned by Mr S Gibbs. The shop front was modernised and enlarged with fittings brought in from Burrows Bros. store in Gold Street, Northampton.*

The shop was later renamed The Post Office Stores by Pauline Bending and continued to sell groceries and stationery. It was later taken over by Alan Wiseman. The Post Office and shop were closed in 2000 and the building converted to a private house in 2004.

The village stores

1 Greenwood's General Stores

Mrs Greenwood and her family arrived in Spratton in 1948 and set up a general stores. Rationing was still in force after the Second World War for some goods such as sweets and chocolates, but supplies were slowly becoming more plentiful. Sugar and dried fruit arrived in large sacks and had to be weighed out into smaller quantities for sale, while butter, lard and margarine came in 28lb blocks.

Mrs Greenwood soon introduced new lines into the shop. Baking tins and mixing bowls went on sale and knitting wools and haberdashery were successful. Later on fruit, vegetables, plants and flowers were added to the stock. Although there were other shops in the village at the time, Greenwood's was the only newsagent. Mrs Greenwood's son, Terry, remembers having to get up early when the newspapers arrived on the first bus at 6.05 am and then doing a paper round before school.

In 1954 *Mrs Greenwood went into partnership with her son. Together they demolished the cottages next door and built a new shop in their place.*

Despite petrol rationing the Greenwoods were able to offer a delivery service three days a week not only to Spratton but also to East Haddon, Guilsborough and Brixworth. They used the back of their 1936 Ford Popular. Creaton Hospital asked for daily newspapers to be delivered to the patients and Cottesbrooke Hall patronised the store. As time went on they ground six different types of coffee bean to order and up to 40 hams at a time were being prepared and cooked by a member of the family.

The Greenwoods finally left the store in 1988 after 40 years in business.

2 Spratton Stores

The store was renamed by the new buyer Alex Crombie when he took over in 1988.

2003 *Spratton Village Store.*

3 Spratton Village Store

Simon Robinson took over the shop in 2000, introduced new lines and changed the name.

Owners of the village shop

Mr E Copson, Mr Moore, Mr Stead, Lillian Gammage 1935, Peter Chapman 1947, Mrs Greenwood 1948, Alex Crombie 1988, Simon Robinson 2000.

Sauls the Butchers

Frank Copson owned the butcher's shop in Brixworth Road until he retired in 1926 and sold the business to Frank Saul. He ran it with his wife, Cecile, and Charles Tipler of Brixworth, a former employee. The property included a slaughterhouse amongst its outbuildings. Cattle and sheep were bought from local farms, pigs were reared and hens were kept in the field on Brixworth Road. Here too cattle were rested before being killed; most weeks one bullock, six sheep and a pig were despatched by Charles Tipler. One eventful day a sheep took fright, ran into the shop and jumped straight through the window.

A pony and trap was used to make deliveries in the early days, but Sauls became the proud owners of a Model T Ford van and also a telephone, one of only four in the village. Deliveries were made to most of the surrounding villages and there was keen competition as most also had a shop. Sauls relied heavily on the custom from the big houses. Mrs Saul made a number of pork pies each week and moulded them by hand on the dining table. They were then taken to Northampton to be baked. Frank Saul's connections with the farming community later brought the custom of the Grand Hotel in Northampton, who provided their kitchen waste for the pigs – often including items of cutlery thrown in by mistake.

In 1933 the business became F E Saul and Sons when the eldest son, Peter, left school. A new van was bought and meat sold directly from the back on a regular round. Times were difficult during the 1939-1945 war with sons Peter and William both joining the forces and also the onset of rationing. Depending on the number of people registering, each shop had a quota of meat plus some corned beef to distribute. Prices were also regulated. Daughter Kathleen was brought in to help with work such as deliveries and book-keeping.

After the war Peter, now married with a small son, Christopher, returned to the shop. Rationing remained until 1954. In the meantime, Frank had been expanding into farming and when Bill was demobbed, they went into dairy farming. History repeated itself when Christopher, after training at Smithfield College and abroad, came into the business. Deliveries were now from a travelling shop. Pork pie production was expanded and many other cooked foods added. More recently, a catering business has been developed. There have been many loyal employees over the years, particularly Yvonne Holmes and Martyn Boshell and the business has grown into the 'Sauls of Spratton' we know today.

2001 *Sauls the Butchers celebrated their 75th anniversary as a family business in 2001*

1934 *The butcher's shop was owned by Frank Saul. Left to right; Kathleen Saul, Cecile Saul, Charles Tipler and Toby, the dog.*

1900 *the butcher's shop in the Brixworth Road was owned by Frank Copson.*

The Corner Shop

To the right is an atmospheric photograph of Spratton in the late 1920s. This is Middle Turn leading into Station Road, now known as the Brixworth Road. The road off to the left is the High Street. The women are standing outside a house which has since been demolished, as has one of the picturesque thatched cottages further down the street. The corner shop, owned by Mr Partridge in 1926, sold groceries, fruit and vegetables and hardware, and in this photograph displays metal advertisements on the walls for products such as Lyons Tea and Sunlight Soap. The house to the right with the open gate was used as a coal merchant's by Frank Cook.

1920s *Brixworth Road, formerly Middle Turn.*

It is known that there was a general store on the corner of the High Street in 1901 when it was owned by Eli James and later by Mr Howlett. The Partridges ran it in 1926 when another store opened up on the other side of the road, just below the site of the present Spratton Stores. In the 1930s the corner shop was owned by the Cory family, followed by Mr and Mrs K Bryant who closed it in 1984. It was then re-opened as a hairdresser by Dawn Mallard in the same year. In 1993, the left hand section was Brown's Bouquets, a florist. This later became a doctor's surgery, an annexe of the Brixworth medical practice.

By 1993 *the corner shop had become a hairdresser's salon with a florist next door.*

1980s *The corner shop was a general grocery store owned by Mr and Mrs Bryant.*

2003 *The hairdresser's shop with a clear view of one of the former thatched cottages. This was part of Thorley's baker's and butcher's shop.*

The King's Head

In the centre of the village, facing the church, stands *The King's Head* public house. The sturdy 17th century stone building with its roof of Welsh slate has in turn been owned by Phipps (from 1960), Watneys and Mann breweries, and is now a freehouse. In the late 20th century the small rooms were opened up into one large room, at one end of which is a preserved well. This would originally have been outside the building but is now contained within an extension. *The King's Head* is thought to stand on the site of a mediaeval hostelry used by visiting clergy from the Abbey of St James in Northampton.

1950s *The main entrance to The King's Head led straight on to the main road. A railing over a small flight of steps prevented drinkers from stumbling out in front of passing traffic.*

1914 *Mr and Mrs Arthur Wood, landlord and landlady of The King's Head from the First World War until the early 1930s. Mr Wood served in the Northampton Regiment in the Great War.*

Landlords of The King's Head until 1982

1849	William Capell
1869	Thomas Davis
	Mrs Mary Davis
1891	William Thompson
1910	A Thomas Green
1914	Arthur J Wood
1930s	Archibald Squires
1940s	Fred Turnell
1953	Jeff Tite
1956	Frank Archer
	Bill Stevens
1959	Ron Lloyd

1925 *The King's Head, a Phipps House selling Phipps Ales and Ratliffes Stouts. The old leaded pane windows are clearly shown.*

The Old Vicarage

The old vicarage stood in its own grounds opposite the church on the corner of Church Road and Brixworth Road (formerly Middle Turn). It was "a neat, brick house" built in 1704 by the vicar of that time, Rev Royle Bateman. It was lived in by the next five vicars until Rev J Llewlyn Roberts brought his young wife to Spratton in 1863. They purchased Spratton House and preferred to use that as the vicarage instead. The old house was leased out to two farmers, first to Andrew Pearson and then to Martin Cotton, before becoming a vicarage again. The present vicarage was built in the 1960s when the old house was demolished.

1930s *The former vicarage, "a neat, brick house" is surrounded by a high wall. It was demolished in the 1960s. To the right are the steps leading to the main entrance of the King's Head, a Phipps house.*

Thatch Cottage & Church, Spratton.

Thatched Stone House

Standing on the corner of Yew Tree Lane is a well-built Grade II listed stone house with a date-stone of 1684 on the side wall. In the 1950s when the top photograph was taken the house had fewer windows than it does today (bottom photograph) and there were no railings outside for the safety of walkers along the footpath leading to the church.

English Martyrs Roman Catholic Church

Yew Tree Lane

After nearly 300 years of persecution and suppression, the Catholic Church restored the hierarchy in England on 29th September 1850. A Bishop was appointed to the new Diocese of Northampton. In 1953 St Patrick's Church, Duston was opened, taking responsibility for the area stretching from Bugbrooke in the south to the Leicester boundary. This included the village of Spratton.

Local people, in particular Mrs Greenwood of Greenwood Stores and Dr Nora O'Leary of Creaton were keen to establish a mass centre in the area and arranged for the purchase of an old army mess hut to be installed on land bought in Yew Tree Lane. This chapel was named English Martyrs and, at the request of the Bishop of Northampton, became the responsibility of the Franciscan order of Greyfriars who had charge of the parish of Duston.

Mass was said every Sunday at 9.00 am by one of the Greyfriars until in the late 1980s when it changed to 5.00 pm. Mass was also said at 7.00 pm on holy days. Typically the weekly mass attendance ran to around 50 people from Spratton and adjoining villages.

In 1991 the Greyfriars vicar-general in England took the decision to reduce the spread of their communities and concentrate the friars in main centres such as London, Manchester and Liverpool. As a result the Bishop of Northampton was forced to close the chapel in Spratton because of the limited number of priests available. The Greyfriars decided that they held the title to the land at Spratton and sold it to the local scout group. The hut remains on Yew Tree Lane and the simple wooden cross above the door is a reminder of its former use in the village.

1966 The wedding of Jillian Green to David Billingham at the Baptist Church on 16th July 1966. The Baptist Chapel was not normally licensed for weddings and special permission had to be granted. Here the bride arrives at the chapel with her father, Leslie Green.

Baptist Chapel

The old Baptist Chapel on the Brixworth Road opposite the church was licensed as a place of worship in 1843. £140 was paid for the building to be used in Trust as a Chapel and Meeting House. The Trustees were William Ekins, William Capell (landlord of *The King's Head*), Richard Baker (a farmer), Thomas Warner (a Baptist Minister), William Adams (a farmer), Richard Letts, Thomas Coleman (a blacksmith), John White (a labourer), Henry Clarke (a shoemaker) and Thomas Lebutt (a brazier).

It was to be "a place of public religious worship for the service of God by Protestant Dissenters called the Independent and Particular Baptists". The first minister was Thomas Warner. Another 19th century minister was James Roach who died in October 1893 aged 42 years. He was buried in the churchyard of St Andrews opposite the chapel.

The chapel was not licensed for weddings, however, and when David Billingham and Jillian Green wished to marry there in 1966 the signatures of all the members of the Chapel had to be obtained in order for permission to be granted.

The chapel was closed early in the 1970s and stood empty for a number of years before being converted to a private house in 1982.

The Bakehouse, Manor Road

During the 19th century there were three bakers in Spratton and this was still the case at the turn of the 20th century. In 1901 John James Muggleton, a young master baker, had taken over William Johnson's bakehouse in Manor Road and continued there for many years. Another young man and master baker, William Thorley, worked from the premises in the Brixworth Road. Both of these bakers were still providing bread for Spratton in the 1920s. At the same time (1901) Thomas Turner and his wife, Agnes, had a bakery and grocer's shop at the Brixworth Road end of Yew Tree Lane. Although Mrs Turner carried on for a few years on her own, the shop had closed by the 1920s.

2003 *The old bakery is a private house today.*

The photograph shows Bert Wykes in 1981 taking a nostalgic look at the old bakehouse in Manor Road which had closed down in 1951. He had started work there as a young lad in 1927 when the baker was Thomas Harris. In those days many people in the village had no ovens at home, so they brought their Sunday dinners to the bakery to be cooked. The cost of cooking a roast dinner with Yorkshire pudding was 2d, a turkey 6d and a cockerel 4d.

1930s *Bert Wykes standing outside the bakehouse in Manor Road.*

The Chequers

The Chequers in Manor Road was once the most popular public house in the village and had a thriving trade until it closed in 1959 supposedly having lost custom because of a lack of car parking space. The building is thought to date back to at least 1630 and the public house was owned by the Northampton Brewery Co. and Phipps in turn. It is now a private house.

In the 19th century it was run for over 60 years by the Pearson family, first William, then his son William and finally by his daughter Sarah. During the Second World War Harry and Gertrude Bannister were the licensees and were hosts to many lively evenings when villagers were joined by soldiers convalescing in the local area. The cellars were used as air raid shelters. The Bannisters' son-in-law, Ron Lloyd, moved on to become landlord of *The King's Head* when *The Chequers* closed.

The house was briefly lived in by the Brooke-Taylor family in the 1970s whose nephew Tim is one of the comedy group the 'Goodies'.

1926 *The Chequers Inn when Albert Gooden was landlord. At that time it belonged to the Phipps Brewery. It stands by a small green in Manor Road.*

(Left) 1902 *One of the oldest photographs of Spratton. The Chequers, a Phipps House, has a thatched roof and the road is unmade.*

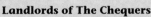

1943 *Harry Bannister, the landlord of The Chequers during the Second World War.*

1940s *Mrs Gertrude Bannister joined the ATS in the Second World War and was a section leader.*

Landlords of The Chequers	
1841	William Pearson
1881	William Pearson Jnr
1890	Miss Sarah Pearson
1901	Edward Cheney
1910	Joseph Marlowe
1920	Albert E Gooden
1940	Harry Bannister
	Closed 1959

Thatched cottages, Manor Road

Opposite *The Chequers* stood a row of picturesque 17th century thatched cottages (shown in the photograph below). The village contained many such dwellings, but just after the Second World War most of them were condemned and demolished. They had one room downstairs and one room upstairs, sometimes divided into two by a curtain. There was no sink as there was no running water to any of the houses in Spratton until the 1950s.

295/3 Erskein Cottages, Spratton

Around the small green outside *The Chequers* stand two substantial stone houses. On the right in the photograph above, is Northbank House, a fine 18th century Grade II listed stone house with a slate roof. Before the Second World War a large upper room was used as a Boys' Club and Peter Saul remembered playing 'shove ha'penny' there. Originally there was a stable block behind the house and when this was demolished, shoe-making equipment was found in the rooms above the stables. Northbank Cottage was added to its left later and had separate occupants until the 1990s when the two properties were joined together.

Water had to be fetched from one of the six public wells or from rainwater butts in the gardens.

In this row there were eight cottages all owned by Lord Erskine of Spratton Hall. Renovation was started sometime in the 1930s when this photo was taken but only two cottages were completed before the rest of the refurbishment was abandoned. Later the remaining cottages were condemned and demolished, only numbers 14 and 16 being left standing. In the 1930s the tenants were: Mrs Hudson, Mrs Roberts, Mrs Lily, the Oldfield family, Walter Wykes, Mrs Martin, Arthur Horne and Bert Wilkes.

On the extreme left of the top photograph one of the Erskine cottages adjoins a thatched stone house with a central front door. Later alterations have blocked out an upstairs window and included another front door.

Manor Road, Then and Now

The photograph above shows Hall Cottages in Manor Road with Home Farm in the distance. The cottages belonged to Spratton Hall and originally were built to house the farm workers. They fell into disrepair and were demolished in the 1950s. The entrance to Tommy Wykes' farm (now the factories) is in the left foreground.

The photograh on the right shows the same section of Manor Road in 2002. Modern private houses have replaced the workers' cottages giving a clear view of the thatched roof of Home Farm, a late 17th century Grade II listed stone house. In 1911 Edward (Teddy) Wykes bought the farmhouse and rented 132 acres of land from Lord Erskine of Spratton Hall, who sometimes went to stay at Home Farm when all his family and staff had gone to his estate in Scotland. The entrance to the leather wholesaler is just beyond the foreground telegraph pole. This was built in the mid 1960s by Peter Lee to deal in leather components and belts.

School Road

There has been a primary school in Spratton (see chapter 7) since 1819 and in the 20th century the road in which it stands was appropriately named School Road. The photograph below shows School Road in the 1930s.

1 Brick house built by Charles Cheney

2 School House, lived in by the schoolmaster Mr G Shaw. Standing back from the road and not shown on the photo is the school itself.

3 White House. An early 17th century building with original 'cruck' beams. It was used by Mrs Dunkley and later Mr Dickens as a grocer's shop and off-license for Phipps Brewery. The house was demolished by order of Brixworth RDC.

4 House owned by Mr Buswell

5 Back entrance to Mr Richardson's shop which sold hardware, groceries and stationery

6 Originally the residential part of the village stores/Post Office, now one of two separate houses

1930s *School Road.*

AROUND THE VILLAGE

Smith Street

At the junction of High Street and Third Turn lived Mr Austin, the shoemaker. In the 19th century a number of families in Spratton took in leather from warehouses in Northampton and produced shoes at home, sometimes in small workshops attached to their houses or in the back gardens. It was often a family affair with mothers and daughters sewing the

uppers and fathers and sons attaching the soles and heels. The craft ran in families and in Spratton the Austins nearly all took to boot and shoemaking. Fathers handed on the skills to their sons and Samuel, William, Frederick, Joseph, Harry, Albert and John Austin are all recorded as being boot and shoemakers in Spratton working at home in the 19th and early 20th centuries. Other families with more than one leather craftsman were the Baldersons, Copsons, Dunkleys, Greens, Higgs and Mannings.

As machines in factories took over from handworkers, village home workshops disappeared. Some shoemakers became shoe repairers but most had closed by the end of the Second World War. The premises shown in the photograph above in Third Turn (now Smith Street) became a private house in the 1950s.

An aerial view of Westaways Garage, Spratton in 2003 (below) and Spratton Service Garage in 1930s (right).

Westaway Motors

Westaways garage in Spratton stands on the A5199 road from Northampton to Leicester and dates from the 1930s when it was run by Griffin and Kingston and known as Spratton Service Garage. In the late 1950s it was taken over by Mr Peter Chapman. In August 1962 it was sold to Westaway Motors Ltd and redeveloped in 1996.

The Rose and Crown

An early photograph (below) of part of Yew Tree Lane shows on the right the former *Bricklayers' Arms* renamed in 1880 *The Rose and Crown*. This public house was owned first by Hipwells Brewery of Olney and then by Phipps Brewery. The landlord was Daniel Hammond followed by his wife Mary after his death in 1894. *The Rose and Crown* was closed in 1922 and was then lived in by Arthur Copson, a poulterer, and the Hammond family who ran a dairy in conjunction with their farm before being sold to the present owner.

The house on the left is called Threeways and is reputed to be built on the oldest foundations in the village. The old Fire Station adjoins it (not shown) and an old well can still be seen in the house. The thatched building in the centre of the photograph is Olde House Farm.

The Fir Tree

At the corner of Holdenby Road and Yew Tree Lane stands *The Fir Tree*, a two storey stone listed Grade II house with a date-stone of 1725 over the front porch. Now a private house, it was formerly an ale house that closed in the early 1950s.

James Pearson was the landlord in 1881 while Henry Catchlove, his wife Sarah and their five children lived there in 1901. Mr and Mrs George Knightall were the landlords in 1910 and Mr and Mrs L Gammage were the last licensees.

1920 *The Fir Tree in Yew Tree Lane.*

Left to right: Threeways, Olde House Farm and the former Rose and Crown. (Date unknown but probably 1930s).

1910 *Mrs George Knightall, the landlady of The Fir Tree.*

29

Cob walls and cottages

One of the distinctive features of Northamptonshire domestic architecture was the use of cob for houses and outside walls. This traditional building material consisted mainly of mud mixed with straw to bind it. Many of the 17th and 18th century cottages and outbuildings in Spratton were made of cob. Although most have now been demolished, some still remain in the village. Cob walls need a firm foundation usually of stone and an overhanging roof of tiles or thatch to protect them from the weather. Thick cob walls keep cottages warm in winter and cool in summer.

2004 *A traditional cob wall round the former estate of Spratton House.*

At the junction of Holdenby Road and Church Road are to be found two remaining examples of the use of cob. The first photograph shows a cob wall built round the former estate of Spratton House. The firm stone foundation and tiled protective roof can be clearly seen. The photograph below shows two thatched cottages with walls of cob. The milk float from Teddy Wykes' dairy and the bunting across the road date the period as probably 1935 (King George V's Silver Jubilee). The premises have been carefully restored and are now one house.

The Rope Walk

Near to the cob cottage at the end of Church Road was the area once known as Rope Walk. Bell ropes and strong agricultural ropes were made here by Spratton rope-makers for churches and farms all around the local area. A wheel supported on two posts was placed at the far end of 'the walk' and to this the rope-maker fastened one end of the hemp which he carried before him. As he walked backwards a child turned the wheel and the rope-maker twisted the hemp into strong and even rope.

1935 *Cottages made of cob (mud and straw) at the corner of Church Road and Holdenby Road.*

During the restoration of the cob cottage large, rounded storage 'caves' were discovered dug out of the earth walls behind the house. Their shape and depth suggest they might have been used to store the hemp and finished ropes.

Chapter Three

THE CHURCH

1984 *The chancel showing Sir John Swinford's tomb and the chantry chapel (now the vestry) beyond. It has been suggested that the unmarked tomb close to the altar is that of Lady Joan Swinford, Sir John's wife and heiress of Sir Thomas Arden. Both the screen and the pulpit had been removed by this date.*

1848 engraving *Spratton Church is by far the oldest building in the village. It was founded in 1120 in the days of Henry I, the son of William the Conqueror. This mid 19th century engraving clearly shows the 14th century south aisle as an extension to the original design. The spire was added to the bell tower in the 15th century.*

Late 19th century *This is an early photograph of the church taken before stained glass was put into the altar window in 1899. There is an elaborate carved screen (now at the back of the church) and a carved wooden pulpit. One of the Norman arches on the north aisle with its richly carved capital can be clearly seen, as well as the Early English pointed arches on the south aisle.*

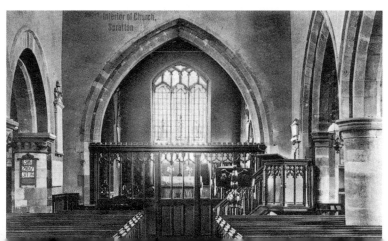

31

2004 *Many people living overseas have ancestors who lived in Spratton. In this photograph Rev Canon Brian Lee shows Natalie Hartwell Lourie and her daughter Diane from New Hampshire, USA, around the church in 2004. They are descended from Thomas Hartwell, vicar of Spratton 1511—1526.*

The elegant metal eagle lectern standing in the chancel has a Latin inscription which translated reads: "To the glory of God and in memory of John Francis Cobb MA thirty six years your constant, faithful and devoted shepherd."

Rev John Cobb was the curate in Spratton when Rev John Bartlett was vicar in the mid 19th century. He lived with his wife Caroline and three surviving children in Church Road and employed at least four servants.

The lectern was restored to its present condition by Mr and Mrs J Cockeram formerly of The Shieling, Church Road.

One of the wooden carvings on the ends of the choir stalls portraying a musician playing a pipe. Other carvings show a bishop and an angel.

The plain stone font situated by the south door is thought to be 13th century or earlier.

Vicars of Spratton

Giles Rous MA		Samuel Denton MA	1613
Archdeacon of Northampton	1269	John Ward MA	1626
Henry de Briggestok	1274	Jonathon Yates	1660
Alfred de Boudon	1278	John Manley LLB	1669
William Brouneye		Royle Bateman MA	1684
Roger Northburgh	1312	William Watson MA	1733
William Holeway de Horle	1345	Christopher Hodgson MA	1738
William Tokey de Wide	1349	William Hughes MA	1776
John, son of William de Grafton	1361	Robert Crowther	1794
John de Adstock		John Bartlett MA	1823
John Martyn	1374	John Llewelyn Roberts MA	1862
John Mallesoures	1377	H G Roberts Hay Boyd MA	1897
William Bate de Kelmarsh	1379	Edmund Oldfield	1906
William Pearsoun		George Raw MA	1907
John Walkelyn	1419	Leslie Vernon Rodgers	1942
John Baxter	1446	Dennis Sidney Pettit	1947
Thomas Parnell	1499	George Thrower	1968
Thomas Hartwell	1511	Clifford Hendey BD	1972
Hugh Witter	1526	Frederick Peter Baker	1978
William Manley	1551	Brian Lee	1984
Robert Clarke	1559		
William Manley	1591		
Richard Butler DD	1591		
Valentine Lane BD	1612		

1966 *Rev Dennis Pettit and Mrs Pettit. Rev Pettit was vicar of Spratton from 1947 to 1968.*

1926 *Rev George Raw and Mrs Raw with their family. Rev Raw was vicar of Spratton from 1907 to 1942.*

1990 *Rev Brian Lee with Mr Robert Parker (United Reform Church) and Father Philip Doughty (Roman Catholic Church). Rev Lee became vicar of Spratton in 1984.*

33

Memorial to Sir John Swinford

One of the treasures of St Andrew's Church is the tomb of Sir John Swinford who died on the Feast of St Stephen (26th December) in 1371. He married Joan, the daughter of Sir Thomas Arden in 1366 and, through her, inherited part of the manor of Spratton.

Their daughter Elizabeth was married at the age of 13 to William de Addebury and later to Roger Chambers. Their descendants continued to hold the manor for many generations..

Sir John is carved in alabaster and the sculptor has finely reproduced the details of his armour. His helmet has a neatly scalloped edge and the tunic, or jupon, is laced at the sides. His belt is buckled at the front and decorated with foliage. His initials J S are repeated three times. From this belt is suspended a large two edged sword. Sir John's feet, in neatly overlapping pieces of protective metal, are resting on a lion. His head is supported by a hollow tilting helmet with a crest showing a boar's head. The whole tomb was originally brightly coloured and traces of paint can be seen around the coats of arms.

The fine detail of the carving of the figure of Sir John Swinford is clearly shown in this photograph. The pattern round the edge of his helmet and the intricacies of the chain mail have been carefully carved. The SS decoration round his neck denotes him as a follower of John of Gaunt, Duke of Lancaster, and is believed to be the earliest representation of this collar in sculpture.

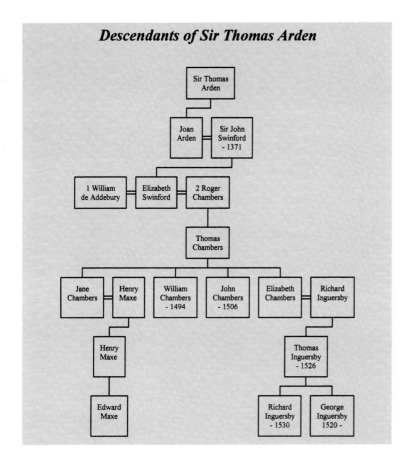

Descendants of Sir Thomas Arden

The family tree of Sir Thomas Arden, showing how the knight, Sir John Swinford married into the family and how his descendants retained this portion of the manor of Spratton for many generations. There is a recorded story that John Chambers (who left money to build the chantry chapel) was furious with the vicar Thomas Parnell and in 1498 accused him of stealing 12 hares, 480 rabbits, 6 pheasants, 100 tench, 300 roach and 100 bream from his land. The vicar denied the charge saying that he had only taken two tench and six roach and in any case John Chambers had given him permission to fish in his pond.

St Andrew's or St Luke's?

The church in Spratton has not always been known as St Andrew's Church, but also as St Luke's Church and plain Spratton Church.

It may originally have been dedicated to St Andrew since three villagers in their wills dated 1510, 1521 and 1528 refer to it as such. However, we know that there were altars in the church to St Barnabas, St Nicholas and St Andrew because in mediaeval times a number of villagers left money to keep candles burning at these altars. Most wills of that time, however, refer to "the church of Sprotton".

Then in the 18th and early 19th centuries, in a series of books about Northamptonshire, "St Luke's Church at Spratton" is mentioned with the additional comment that "there is a vacant place in the south aisle of the church where the statue of St Luke formerly stood." When and why this change of dedication took place is not known.

The Parish Registers in the 20th century refer to St Luke's Church until 1949 when Rev D Pettit changed the dedication to St Andrew, on the basis of the three mediaeval wills and the fact that the authoritative Victoria County History gave St Andrew as the dedication. The official change was made between 8th October 1949 and 27th December 1949, possibly on St Andrew's day on 30th November.

Walter Bolekek, sanctuary seeker

Another mediaeval story concerns a Spratton man, Walter Bolekek, a self-confessed thief. Rather than be put to death for his crimes, in 1329 he sought sanctuary in Spratton church. Here he was safe for 40 days, according to the law at that time. He then took an oath to leave the country for ever. Leaving the church in sackcloth, bare-footed and with a wooden cross in his hands, he made his way to the nearest port. Constables supervised him every step of the way and he had to take the first ship that sailed. Walter left behind a small number of goods and chattels which the men of Spratton divided up among themselves. The Abbot of St James took over his small piece of land and was promptly fined 40 pence for so doing! The law of sanctuary for those accused of crimes was not abolished until 1623.

The Bells

The five old bells in Spratton Church were originally cast in a wooden frame in 1685 by Matthew and Henry Bagley who were later killed when a bell mould full of molten metal exploded.

In 1929 the vicar, Rev George Raw, received the bad news that the old bells needed to be rehung in a steel frame and No 2 and No 4 bells had to be recast. Rev Raw reminded the village how important the bells were and how they had rung out over the centuries for great national occasions. He mentioned the old village records showing 2 shillings had been paid to the Spratton bell ringers when we had the victory in Flanders. This was in 1706 when the Duke of Marlborough was victorious over the French at the Battle of Ramillies, Flanders, in the War of the Spanish Succession. In 1714 they rang out again when the king landed and the ringers were paid 10 shillings.

George I, having succeeded Queen Anne, travelled from Hanover, Germany, and landed in England to national rejoicing. The bells rang out again for the coronation of George I – a grand day according to the old records – and 4 shillings was paid to the ringers.

The work on the bells was carried out by John Taylor of Loughborough. People in the village responded well to the vicar's request for donations and the cost of £385 was soon met. On Tuesday 8th April 1930 the Bishop came to dedicate the newly

1988. The new sixth bell *On one side is inscribed RIP Harry Bannister 1880—1959, Brian Lee—Vicar , Humphrey H Bennett, B Joan Savage—Wardens. On the other side is inscribed Bellringers C William Brown, Kirsty A Gascoin, Jon Spencer (Capt), Pamela M Spencer, David J Spencer, M J Bill Blowfield, Tania Blowfield, Stephen M Jones.*

restored bells and a team of Diocesan Guild of Church Bell Ringers under the Master, Mr F Wilford, brought out the music of the bells.

1988 *Irene Eaton, daughter of Harry Bannister, who made a major donation towards the cost of the new bell in memory of her father.*

1988 *William Brown aged 87 years was first to ring the new sixth bell when it was installed.*

The bells were re-installed in a six-bell frame leaving a spare space for a new bell in the future. A new treble bell weighing five and a quarter hundredweight was installed in 1988 and rung for the first time by C William Brown, better known as Bill. Bill Brown was taught bell ringing by his father in 1911 when he was 10 years old and he continued ringing until old age. He was captain of the Spratton bell-ringers and also Master of the Guilsborough Branch of the Diocesan Guild of Church Bell Ringers.

The sixth bell was cast by Eijsbouts of Holland and installed by Eayre and Smith Ltd of Melbourne, Derby. It cost nearly £4,000 and was paid for by generous donations. The largest of these was given in memory of another Spratton bell-ringer, Harry Bannister, who died in 1959 aged 79 years. The new bell was designed with the help of a computer analysis of the tones of the old bells.

1929 *The five old church bells, originally installed in 1685, were taken out of the church tower for restoration in 1929.*
Left to right: Edward Austin, William Buswell, Charles Gilby, Arthur Balderson, Rev George Raw, George Payne, Thomas Manning and sitting
William Balderson.

Spratton villagers have been buried in the churchyard for nearly 800 years and thousands lie beneath the grass. Today, only 215 graves are marked with tombstones mainly from 18th and 19th centuries. The churchyard was closed for burial in 1903.

Repairs and Restoration

Over the years the vicars and parishioners of Spratton have made sure their church has been kept in good repair. There was major restoration in 1846-47 under the superintendence of G C Scott. In the early part of the 20th century the Rev George Raw sent out appeals for donations to repair both the spire and the roof. Two terrible storms in 1938 and 1946 badly damaged the spire and people reported that the church looked as if a bomb had hit it after the lightning damage of 1946.

Electricity had been installed in 1928 and by 1984 the whole church had to be re-wired. It was re-decorated at the same time thanks to a generous legacy from a parishioner. In 1986 more money was needed to repair the windows and in 1987 major fund-raising was carried out to restore the tower. English Heritage provided 60% of the necessary finance and the rest (£50,000) was raised from appeals to grant-making charities and from many fund-raising events in the village. A Service of Thanksgiving was held in January 1990 when Rev Brian Lee dedicated all the restoration work carried out over the last six years.

1990 *On 4th February 1990, after the morning service, Rev Brian Lee removed the sign about the danger of falling masonry which had been in place for 20 years.. This marked the end of a long and difficult project to restore the ancient tower.*

In 1998 *more fund-raising was undertaken in order to repair drainage, re-lead windows and treat the roof timbers. Again money was raised from both charitable grants and major events in the village. In the photograph below Sir John Lowther presents a cheque for £2,000 towards church restoration to Enid Jarvis of the Friends of St Andrew's Church on behalf of the Northamptonshire Historic Churches Trust. The presentation, to Spratton and a number of other local churches, took place in Titchmarsh on 6th July 1998.*

The Churchyard Cross

On the south side of the churchyard stand the remains of a small churchyard cross. It has a square stepped base and the octagonal shaft is set into the top step. The base of the shaft appears to be decorated with carvings. The shaft is slender and tapers towards the top where there is an incised line. The arms of the cross would have fitted in here but no longer exist.

For many years it was thought that this was a mediaeval preaching cross used by travelling friars and that perhaps it had been moved to the churchyard at a later date. However, in 2003 the cross was renovated and, under the guidance of the church architect and English Heritage, it was carefully taken to pieces. The foundations were found to be mediaeval and almost definitely in their original position, so the cross had not been moved here from elsewhere. Further research revealed that there are very few preaching crosses left in England and none in Northamptonshire. Apparently stone crosses were raised in many churchyards throughout the land in the years before the Reformation. They were generally placed to the south-east of the south door so that all should see the cross on entering the church and be inspired with reverence for the service in which they were about to take part. The cross in Spratton churchyard is in this exact position. It also served as a station or stopping place for outdoor processions, particularly on Palm Sunday. After the palms had been distributed, the procession moved out of the church towards the cross with the choir singing anthems telling the biblical story of Palm Sunday.

In the reign of Henry VIII's son, the Protestant Edward VI, the mediaeval altars in parish churches were removed together with lights, images and wall paintings. All the colourful vestments, sacred vessels and ornaments were confiscated. Is this perhaps when the head of the cross in Spratton churchyard was removed and smashed?

2003 *The 14th century churchyard cross before and after restoration.*

2003 *During restoration mediaeval foundations were found beneath the churchyard cross. Concrete was poured onto the unevenground in the centre to make a firm base for the newly restored plinth and shaft.*

1996 *The Friends of St Andrew's Church raised the money for a commemorative plaque to Amphillis Twigden to be placed near the font where she was baptised. On 30th October 1996 Laurence Tuck, a visitor from the USA was invited to unveil the plaque which was then dedicated by Rev Canon Brian Lee. The flower arrangement was created with an American theme by Frances Roseblade.*

1996 *The stonemason carefully puts the commemorative plaque to Amphillis Twigden and the Washingtons into position.*

The Washington Connection

George Washington (1732-1799) first President of the United States was descended from notable Northamptonshire families. His great-great grandfather was Rev Lawrence Washington who was born at Sulgrave Manor and his great-great grandmother was Amphillis Twigden who was born in the parish of Spratton at Little Creaton; she was baptised in Spratton Church on 2nd February 1602. The 13th century font is still in use today.

Her father was John Twigden, a member of a well-to-do and highly respected local family. Her two uncles, John's brothers Edward and Ralph, also lived in Spratton. Edward the elder brother and his family are commemorated by a brass in Spratton Church. The brass tells us that Edward and his wife Ann both died in 1614 and that they left three daughters, Elizabeth, Bridgett and Ann.

Amphillis' mother was Anne Dickons from Greater Creaton. After the death of her husband in 1610 when Amphillis was eight years old, Anne married Andrew Knowling from Tring in Hertfordshire and took her children to live in her new home. Anne died in Tring in 1637.

John and Lawrence, two sons of Lawrence Washington and Amphillis Twigden, decided to try their luck overseas and after the death of their parents left England for the colonies in America arriving in Virginia in 1657 with a number of other wealthy emigrants from Northamptonshire. The brothers prospered and in 1674 Lieutenant Colonel John Washington acquired 5,000 acres of wilderness at the confluence of Little Hunting Creek and the Potomac River. His partner was a distant relative from Northamptonshire, Colonel Nicholas Spencer.

John Washington's share of the land, later named Mount Vernon, in due course descended to George Washington, who in 1776 became first president of the newly independent United States. Here, he made his home with his wife Martha and after his death at the age of 67 in 1799 he was buried in the family tomb on the estate.

THE LARGE HOUSES

Spratton Hall

Spratton Hall, (also known as Spratton Place), the largest house in the village, is a plain, three storey, 18th century structure made of limestone (from Kingsthorpe) and roofed with slates. The date 1773 is marked on the rainwater leads, although the house was probably built in 1760 on the site of an earlier farmhouse. Despite the fact that a number of extensions and additions were carried out in the 19th and 20th centuries, the house has a Grade II listing.

It was built by Francis Beynon who, through marriage and successive small purchases, had acquired a considerable estate locally. At the time of Spratton's Inclosure Award 1766 he had a claim to just under 300 acres of farm land mainly in Bridge Field and the South Ryefield. The ornate marble memorial plaque installed in the church by his only surviving child, Elizabeth, calls him 'the best of fathers' and records that he died in 1778 aged 62 years. The land, by then 520 acres, and house were inherited by Elizabeth's son, Francis Beynon Hackett who lived at Moor Hall, Sutton Coldfield, Warwickshire. He did not come to live in Spratton.

Robert Ramsden was the next owner of Spratton Hall. He arrived as a young man in 1818 with his wife Frances and sister-in-law Annabella Helen Plumtre. Six children were born to the Ramsdens in the next 11 years. They were all baptised in Spratton Church and sadly three were buried there as well. The grieving

1946 *Preparations for the summer fete at Spratton Hall.*

parents erected memorials to them all inside the church. Mr and Mrs Ramsden played an active part in village life until they moved to the family seat of Carlton Hall, Nottinghamshire in 1831.

They took a great interest in education and, together with the vicar, the Rev Robert Crowther, and the schoolmaster Mr John Pridmore, helped to put Spratton far ahead of its neighbours educationally. Robert Ramsden endowed a Free School for Girls and Boys and also an Infants School.(See page 62) Mrs Ramsden and her sister ran the Spratton Ladies' Bible Association providing Bibles for the poor of the village for a few pence. The Rev Thomas Jones, curate of Spratton, wrote in his memoirs, *In the year 1818, it pleased God to bring into that Parish [Spratton] a family which has been a great help and comfort to me, and an immense benefit to the parish, and to the whole neighbourhood to a considerable extent. I allude to Robert Ramsden, Esquire; who continued to reside there for 13 years. Schools and religious institutions were established and conducted by him; and he derived no small assistance from his invaluable sister-in-law, Miss Plumtre, and from Mrs Ramsden. Such a family I never expect to see again, whose only and constant aim was to do good, to serve God, and their generation.*

1940s Spratton Hall

The entrance hall has an 18th century Adam style fireplace and beautiful staircase above which is an elegant glazed arched screen.

1956 *An aerial view of Spratton Hall taken from the back over the lawn and the gardens. The front of the house and the main drive is partially hidden.*

large part in the life of the village for many years, supporting events and giving generous donations to worthy causes such as the restoration of the church and the elementary school as well as the tea parties for the Mothers' Union. Lady Erskine raised funds for the street lighting in the village until she left in September 1915. She earnestly hoped someone else would take over her role. She wrote, *I am such a believer in light and the good it effects in villages.....It will make me so unhappy to think my dear Spratton, where I have spent so many long and happy years, should be left in darkness.* The 5th Baron Erskine died at the Hall in 1913 aged 72 years and his wife, who was in poor health, left Spratton in 1915 and died in 1922. They are both commemorated with memorial plaques in the church. The 6th Baron Erskine sold the Hall and estate in 1936 to Mr Ernest Byng and the farm was let out to Edward (Teddy) Wykes in 1941 (owner of Home Farm. See page 52).

In 1945 the Hall was auctioned and bought by Mr and Mrs Phipps (Phipps' Brewery) who sold it in 1947 to the Cazenove family for £10,000. By this time the estate included a farm, seven cottages and 137 acres of land. The Darling family acquired the estate two years later.

In 1951 Kenneth and Joan Hunter bought the house and turned it into a successful school. It is now an independent preparatory school for boys and girls aged 7 – 13 years. The actor Tenniel Evans taught English and Drama there for a short time in the early 1950s before returning to the theatre. He played regularly with the Northampton Repertory Theatre. Matt Dawson, the Saints and England rugby player, was a teacher there from 1996 to 1997.

Another early tenant was General Whichcote who lived in the house in the 1840s. He was notable in the village for having fought in the Battle of Waterloo in 1815. He also attended the famous officers' ball given by the Duchess of Richmond in Paris on the night before the battle. When he died in 1891, having left Spratton long before, some villagers claimed to remember him, 'a fine, portly figure' walking around the village with a basket on his arm full of good things for the sick. He would visit the poor and the elderly to read to them and people remembered his 'frank and courteous bearing and his kind and unfailing liberality.'

By 1849 the Hall was the property of Captain Mildmay Clerk RN and a gravestone in the churchyard marks his death in 1877 aged 66 years.

Captain Theophilus Gist, formerly of the 7th Hussars, had bought the Hall and estate by 1881, and lived there with his wife and young son, Frank, selling it to William Macnaghten, the 5th Baron Erskine in 1890. Lord Erskine had served in the Queen's 9th Royal Lancers mainly in Ireland from 1860 to 1869 when he retired in the rank of captain. After that he spent many years in the legal profession. By the time he bought Spratton Hall, Lord Erskine was 50 years of age, his wife Lady Alice was 46 and their son Montague was 25. Lord and Lady Erskine played a

1896 *A pencil sketch showing Lady Erskine playing cards with Mr Langham. A small book of pencil drawings made by a lady at Spratton Hall was passed to a senior servant as a gift and still survives in her family.*

1946 *The 6th Baron Erskine buys a tombola ticket from Mrs Flint at the summer fete in 1946.*

1940s *The garden of Spratton Hall.*

1896 *More sketches by the same artist either of members of the Erskine family or some of their house guests.*

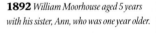

1892 *William Moorhouse aged 5 years with his sister, Ann, who was one year older.*

Spratton Grange

Spratton Grange was built in 1847 as a hunting lodge in 246 acres of land just outside Spratton village. We know that in 1849 it was occupied by the Dowager Lady St John and then by Mr A Berens in 1875. In 1878 it was given to W Henry Foster whose family were wealthy coal mine owners in Shropshire. His wife, Henrietta, was Irish and a woman of considerable wealth, accomplishments and culture. Henry Foster enlarged the house for his growing family (3 daughters and a son) and generously agreed to pay for the clock in the Spratton church tower to be installed in 1886. The family left Spratton when Mr Foster's father died and he had to return to the family seat in Apsley, Shropshire. He did not sell Spratton Grange but let it out to tenants for a number of years.

The first tenant was the very wealthy Edward Moorhouse who came with his New Zealand born wife in 1901. At that time they had two teenage daughters, Ann and Mary who were educated at home by a governess (who was later to become a well-known suffragette. See page 14), and two sons, William away at Harrow and Edward who was 7 years old. The family kept a large staff of at least 12 servants as well as gardeners, grooms, stable-hands and a coachman. Mrs Moorhouse and her daughters played an active part in village life, helping Lady Erskine run a girls' club and throwing open the gardens of the Grange for village functions. In 1911 Mary sent a letter to all the girls named Mary in the village asking them for a contribution to a coronation gift for their namesake, the new Queen Mary. The family always headed the list of subscribers when money was needed for worthy causes such as the school building fund and the village street lighting. Indeed Mrs Moorhouse sent generous donations for the church bells and repair of the church roof long after leaving the village in 1915. The Moorhouse family have been rather over-shadowed by their eldest son William who was 14 years old when they first came to Spratton. While at school at Harrow he developed a passion for speed and the workings of the

c 1912 *William Moorhouse at home at Spratton Grange.*

internal combustion engine. He is remembered in the village between 1909 and 1914 for his many motor cars in which he used to race around the streets with local boys on board. Sidney Holt said William tested his cars on the hill leading up to Holdenby and he used to get Sid's father and his brothers to sit in the back to give more weight. Even more exciting for everyone, however, was his flying machine which local mechanics would work on with amazement. Arthur Branson said, "The first aeroplane I saw was flown by Billy Moorhouse. He gave us a thrill when he flew low over the school one day. We all ran down to the Grange to see this wonderful machine that could fly. That was in 1911. Everyone in the village was there." William was the first person in Northamptonshire to learn to fly and he went on to distinguish himself in the Royal Flying Corps in the First World War as the first airman ever to be awarded a Victoria Cross. He died of his wounds in 1915. (See pages 71 and 72)

The next tenant allowed the Grange to deteriorate badly. There are stories that even chickens were found wandering through the house and nesting in the Billiard Room.

Henrietta Foster returned to the Grange in the 1920s after her husband died and their son, Arthur, took over the family house in Shropshire. She had extensive work done on the house to restore it and lived in some style with a staff of 13 as well as keeping a chauffeur driven Daimler. She gave generously to requests for donations to village causes and was sadly missed when she died in 1939 aged 90 years. The vicar, the Rev George Raw wrote, *Her thought for the sick and poor and her manifold kindness to them, her ready help for every good cause and her interest in all that concerned the welfare of the parish are things that will not soon be forgotten. She recognised the responsibility as well as the privilege of wealth.* In 1955 the frame of the bells in the church tower was repaired in her memory.

During the Second World War the Grange was occupied by the Army for five years, some 200 to 300 men being billeted

Mrs Henrietta Foster and her family in the gardens at Spratton Grange. Her grand-daughter, Rebecca Belben sits with her mother on the rug. When she was older she helped in the village with the Girl Guides company.

in the grounds. The water they used was pumped up from a spring. After the war the house was auctioned with 246 acres and the new owner, Dr Starkey, pulled down the wings and extensions to make the property more manageable. In the 1960s the estate was broken up and sold in lots. The stables were converted to a smaller house, the farmland sold separately and the Grange, lodge and eight acres of land sold to a new owner.

1915 *William Rhodes-Moorhouse, his wife Linda, and son William, at Spratton Grange shortly before he was killed in action.*

1946 *Spratton Grange.*

Broomhill

1935 *Broomhill when it was owned by the Manningham-Buller family.*

The ancient name 'Broomhill' refers to the broom and gorse that grew profusely in the sandy soil in the western part of the village. In fact it became a custom on the Monday following Spratton Feast Sunday for villagers to walk up to the hill together to gather gorse from the common land and take it home to use as fuel.

The large house named Broomhill standing on the outskirts of the village was designed by the architectural firm of Goddards in Leicester and although the deeds were lost in a fire in a London solicitor's office during the Second World War, the architect's drawings exist dating from 1869 and 1871. The house can also be dated from a large stone near the back porch to 1872. It was built by Colonel Henry de Tessier.

By 1881 it was owned by Francis Bruce Simson, who had lived in India for most of his life and had recently retired from HM Bengal Civil Service. He lived in the house with his wife and young son, Bruce, and five or six servants.

When Sir Mervyn Manningham-Buller, Speaker of the House of Commons and MP for Daventry, bought the

house in 1902 the property consisted of the main house run by 12 staff, a cottage, a coach house, stables, grooms' quarters and a farm cottage, Spratton Lodge, for a farm manager together with about 150 acres of farm land. Sir Mervyn had the original staircase removed and replaced with a pine and mahogany one that had come from Burlington House. Sir Mervyn's son, Lord Dilhorn, later also became an MP as well as Lord Chancellor and his grand-daughter, Elizabeth, became head of MI5.

The house was sold around 1928 to a speculator who hoped to sell at a profit. Unfortunately the economic conditions of the time meant that house prices fell and Broomhill remained unsold and empty for seven years.

Later in 1935 *after the Church family had modernised the house. The downstairs bay windows at the back of the house were altered by taking out the heavy stone mullions to give more light to the rooms inside.*

Christopher Kench, the former head gardener, who made floral garlands for the children's May Day celebrations, looked after the house until it was sold in 1935 to Leslie Church, the Chairman of Church and Co., shoe manufacturers. The Church family made many improvements to modernise the house, including installing a huge central heating system.

During the war Mr and Mrs Church moved into the groom's quarters and in 1941 let the main house to Blagdens, a small firm from London who had been bombed out of their offices. Blagdens came with all their staff and stayed until Broomhill became an annexe to Northampton General Hospital in June 1943. Here patients were able to recuperate after their operations. After June 6th 1944 only military patients were admitted and Mrs Church, a VAD, was able to help with the nursing. The house took a maximum of 40 soldiers and the regime was strict. There is a story that some of the soldiers escaped by climbing down the wisteria from the upper bedrooms and walking across the fields for a drink in *The Chequers* in Spratton.

In 1946 Mr Church sold Broomhill to the influential Sir John Pascoe, managing director of British Timken. He was an enthusiastic supporter of cricket and football in the village and Lady Pascoe also enjoyed contributing to village life. The Kench family were tenant farmers here in the 1940s. Sir John sold the house in 1961 to Humphrey Bennett, a highly respected local property manager and in 1979 it changed hands again when it was bought by Mr Featherstone. Finally, in 1984 it was sold to Joe Kelly who later turned it into a successful country hotel.

1920s *Charles Branson, farm manager for Sir Mervyn Manningham-Buller at Broomhill.*

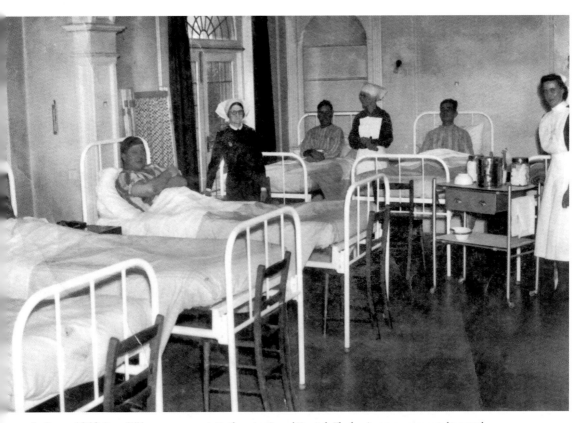

In June 1943 *Broomhill became an annexe to Northampton General Hospital. The drawing room was converted to a ward.*

Spratton House

A plaque commemorating Thomas Butlin who lived at Spratton House. He financed the beginnings of the Northamptonshire iron industry which was continued and developed by his son, William (born 1824). William established the firm of Thomas Butlin Co. opening a Vulcan foundry in Western Avenue, Northampton, around 1845 and a second blast furnace in a new works in Irthingborough in 1867.

Thomas's brother, Edward (born 1793), lived at Holly House next door with his wife and daughter and continued with the family's wool trade interests after Thomas had diversified into iron and engineering. After a serious family disagreement Thomas blocked up the gateway between the two properties and raised the low brick wall to a height of 12 feet. Both brothers are buried in the churchyard and their families put up elaborate memorial plaques to them in the church.

In 1864 the Rev Llewelyn Roberts who had become vicar of Spratton two years earlier, bought Spratton House. Rev Roberts had decided that the old vicarage was not suitable for his needs and he moved his wife and three young daughters, Georgina, Edith and Margaret, into Spratton House together with their governess and four servants. Canon Roberts was held in affectionate esteem by the village and a stained glass window was erected in the church in his memory in 1899. Mrs Roberts played an active part in village life and was mainly responsible for reviving the dying lace industry in Spratton. Mrs Roberts died in 1928 after 65 years in the village and is buried with her husband in the churchyard.

Spratton House dates from 1793 when it was built by William Butlin as a home for his growing family and in a style appropriate to his importance in the local neighbourhood. The Butlin family was highly respected in Spratton and had been so from the end of the 16th century. As considerable landowners in the area, they seemed also to have acted as local financiers and entrepreneurs. Their main business, however, was wool.

In the depression of the post-war Napoleonic era of the 1840s, the Butlin family's fortunes thrived despite a downturn in the wool industry. Realising that the best times for wool had passed, they turned their attention elsewhere and William's son, Thomas (born 1792), developed and financed the family's expansion into the iron industry. Thomas Butlin and his family lived at Spratton House with two servants and a young groom.

Following Canon Roberts' death in 1898 Mrs Roberts and her daughters moved and Spratton House was sold to Mildred and Ulrica Bevan, the daughters of Richard Lee Bevan of Brixworth Hall. People still remember that the sisters expected to be treated with great respect as befitted their social position in the village and would report any schoolchildren who did not curtsey or raise their caps to them. They maintained at least five staff (cook, parlour maid, housemaid and kitchen maid) and four outdoor staff housed in the cottages they owned (now Mulberry Cottage in Yew Tree Lane, but then three separate cottages).

They responded generously to the vicar's constant requests for donations and acted as local benefactors in a number of ways, including paying for the repair of the chancel floor in the church. During the First World War they made part of the house available as a convalescent home for wounded officers and presented a Roll of Honour of Spratton men who enlisted in the Great War to the church. They contributed generously to the cost of the War Memorial and in a photograph (unfortunately of very poor quality) of the dedication of the War Memorial in 1921, they can just be seen, then in their late 60s, standing at the front of the crowd of villagers holding themselves very upright and stiffly. When Miss Ulrica died in 1940 the vicar wrote of her, *Reserved by nature, she shunned all publicity and her many kindnesses were always done unobtrusively and without any fuss.*

The subsequent owners of the house, Sir Rupert and Lady Hardy, who sold off parts of the estate before they moved away, are still remembered in the village.

1965 Holly House

Holly House and two cottages (since demolished) are shown in the foreground with part of Spratton House in the background on the left. Mr Shaw, headteacher of the village school, lived at Holly House in the 1930s and 1940s.

In the centre background are the staff cottages for Spratton House with their gardens. These have now been refurbished as one house.

1960s *An aerial view of 1 Spratton House (centre) and its surroundings drawn in the 1960s. 2 The Shieling can just be seen in the trees in front of Spratton House. 3 Cotfield with its long barn stands out clearly. In the left fore-ground is 4 Threeways and left of Spratton House are the coach house 5 and three staff cottages. 6 Holly House and its cottages stand on the back right of the drawing.*

Fig. 11. Aerial view of Spratton House (marked with arrow) and surroundings, showing the Staff Cottage at the rear. From a photograph taken in the 1960s.

The Manor House, Church Road.

The Manor House
Church Road

This old house standing opposite the church has wooden beams inside that date it back to the 17th century. It originally had a thatched roof which was blown off in a terrible storm in 1905. After this the roof was slated and the old leaded windows with stone mullions were replaced with modern sash windows. Behind the house there stood formerly a dovecote with 1,600 nesting boxes. It had belonged in mediaeval times to the Abbey of St James in Northampton to enable them to 'support a more extended hospitality.' The dovecote was pulled down around 1890 and the stones used in constructing a new lodge near Holdenby House.

The Copson family bought the Manor in 1870 at which time it was one long house with the entrance at the back. From 1874 to 1916 the Copsons ran the Post Office and to make the handling of post bags easier an entrance was made at the front of the house.

The Manor House
Manor Road

Next door to *The Chequers* in Manor Road is another house named Manor House. It was at some time called Kites Hall

until it was occupied in the 1890s by the Rev Humphrey G Roberts, the curate of Spratton and later the vicar. He changed the name from Kites Hall to the Manor House. The vicar seems to have been fond of changing names as he changed his own name to Humphrey G Roberts Hay-Boyd when he married Mary Hay-Boyd. He remained in Spratton for 11 years, donating a stained glass window to the church in 1906.

2003 *The Lantsbery family tomb in St Andrew's Churchyard.*

In the 19th century the house was owned by the Lantsbery family, people of considerable substance locally owning farms in Ravensthorpe and Creaton as well as property in Spratton. William Lantsbery 1751-1821 and his wife, Alice 1761-1831, were members of the Creaton Independent Chapel and their first four children were baptised there between 1799 and 1805. In 1806 it was decided to build a chapel in Spratton for the freedom of worship for Protestant dissenters and William Lantsbery donated land and stone to supplement Creaton Chapel's cash. The chapel was built next to the Lantsbery family home. Alice Lantsbery wrote in the Chapel bible, *Began to build this meeting house in our orchard June 27th 1806 and it was built by subscription and collected by Mr Whitehead. My dear Mr William Lantsbery gave the ground and stone to build the east side and boarded the men whilst in building it. Opened it the day I was 30 years old September 27th 1806.* It is somewhat surprising to find this Non-Conformist family buried in such a prominent grave in the Established Church.

William and Alice's son, William 1802-1884, a prosperous farmer, lived at the family home and married three times. He took a lively part in village politics and showed great concern for the plight of the poor. As a dying man he was admitted to membership of the independent church on 2nd January 1884. He died on 18th January. By 1893 the Chapel had fallen into disuse and it was sold for £40 to Mr Gulliver, the new owner of the Manor House.

Two William Lantsberys had lived in this house for many years and the road adjoining the property to the rear became known, rather disrespectfully for the times, as Billy Lantsbery's Backside.

The independent chapel built on William Lantsbery's land in Spratton as a place of worship for Protestant dissenters.

Chapter Five

FARMING

Since earliest times people in Spratton have relied heavily on the land for their living and their way of life. The pattern of local farms began to take shape after the Spratton Inclosure of land in 1766 with the Church and the estate at Spratton Hall owning extensive acreage.

In the 19th century agriculture accounted for most of the jobs for working men (see page 13), only being overtaken by other occupations when machinery reduced the number of men needed on the farms and higher wages elsewhere tempted them away from the land.

Broomhill

Charles Branson was the farm manager for Sir Mervyn Manningham-Buller on the Broomhill estate, and his son Arthur, remembers his happy childhood growing up on the farm in the early 1900s.

"We all had to take our turn at the different farm work like milking the cows. When the war (First World War) started, men were hard to get for farm work, so we boys had to take up the slack. One of my regular jobs was to take a gallon of milk each morning and evening to the big house. I did that for a long time and liked the job; I was well looked after by the staff. The cooks always had a treat for me......

Hay time and harvest were great days. Help would come from the stable hands at haying time. About four in the afternoon we boys would go to the estate kitchen where the cook would have prepared a basket of sandwiches and cake, and a can of tea. We would all then sit down in the field and enjoy our tea break. All hay and grain was put in stacks at the farm, then once each year, a steam engine would come puffing in hauling the threshing machine and stacker. It would take some time to get all lined up with the driving belts in place. We would sit and watch with amazement at the skill of the driver with the big lumbering steam engine....

The war years changed everything for us. I was 12 years old when it started in 1914. Most of the young fellows in the village joined the army right away and it soon got to the point where very few men were left to work on the farms so we boys had to help the best we could. After a while a prisoner of war camp was set up on a farm just north of Creaton. The prisoners had all volunteered to work on the farms. I saw my first Germans as they came marching through the village with two British soldiers as guards with their guns and fixed bayonets. There were about 20 of them in their grey uniforms and pillbox hats and a big red patch on their backs and on each trouser leg. Dad had three for just over two years. They were good workers and anxious to please. At first Dad had to go and get them from the camp each morning and return them to camp each night. After awhile we boys were allowed to be the guards and it became my job to go for them each morning and take them back at night. War is a stupid thing. There was my brother, uncles and cousins over in France fighting the Germans, and we had three who had become our friends and who, but for going back to the camp each night, were free and enjoying working on the farm."

1920s *Arthur Branson, son of Charles Branson who was farm manager of Broomhill Farm in the early years of the 20th century.*

Home Farm

Thomas Manning farmed here before 1911 when Edward (Teddy) Wykes bought the farmhouse and land, including the field now known as the Recreation Field. He also rented 132 acres from Lord Erskine of Spratton Hall and land from the Bosworth family up to Teeton brook. In the 1930s he was running a mixed farm, both arable and animals (poultry, pigs, 1,000 sheep). He had two permanent farm hands: Dick

1996 *Home Farm after rethatching.*

Wykes (a nephew) and William Manning. During the Second World War they were helped by four prisoners of war, billeted at Boughton, who were brought in every day under guard.

1930s *Haymaking at Home Farm.*
Back row: Sidney Wykes, Harry Wykes, Jack Martin, George Pateman, Edward (Teddy) Wykes.
Front row: Albert Wilkes, Charles Wilkes with Arsy the dog, Dick Wykes with his dog Peter, Thomas Cook.

1940s *Edward (Teddy) Wykes who farmed at Home Farm for many years.*

1930s *Threshing time at Home Farm —an atmospheric picture recalling bygone days. The traction engine came from Sonny Rose at Brixworth. Dick Wykes with his dog Peter are sitting by the machine with farmer, Edward Wykes. Two of the children are thought to be Janet Cotterell and Angela Summerford.*

1965 *Gilby's Farm in Yew Tree Lane (A) lies on the right hand side of this aerial photograph. In the yard adjacent to the house are the old granary, the new granary built over the stables, a big loose-box for calves, and a barn. Further east was another yard with two pig sties, and a rickyard with a four-bay Dutch barn.*

Gilby's Farm

The farmhouse on Gilby's farm dates back to the early 17th century. It was owned by Richard Gilby in the 1880s. His son, Arthur, farmed here until he died in 1932 aged 53 years and was followed by his son Charles. Charles sold the farm in the 1950s.

1930s *Charles Gilby's wife Stella (nee Busby) and sister Mary at lambing time on the farm.*

1937 *Gilby family group taken at the christening of Charles and Stella Gilby's son Richard.*

Back row: Charles Gilby (father), Edward Turney, Edward Busby (grandfather), Monty Marriott, Rosa Gilby (Alfred Gilby's daughter).

Front row: Thomas Puttnam, Stella Gilby (mother), Mrs Alfred Gilby (holding Richard), Helen Busby (grandmother), Jane Sheppard, Mary Gilby, Mrs Monty Marriott, John Sheppard, Frank Saul, Cecile Saul.

Charles Gilby

In the mid 1930s Gilby's Farm was mainly pastureland for cattle and sheep but by the 1950s it produced crops of wheat, barley and oats and kept poultry and pigs as well.

In its day it was the largest and most up-to-date farm in Spratton covering 351 acres. During the Second World War they employed live-in land girls while German and Italian prisoners of war were brought in at harvest time.

Alfred Gilby, Arthur's brother, ran a smaller farm and dairy in Yew Tree Lane known as 'Top' farm while the larger farm was 'Bottom' farm. Alfred died in 1931 aged 56 years.

Scale 6" = 1 mile

N

1960s *An aerial view of Grange Farm with the farmhouse in the foreground.*

1935 *Grange Farm.*

Grange Farm

Spratton Grange was a mixed farm when Harry Hammond became the tenant in 1925. He farmed there for ten years before Lewis Morgan and his wife Mary Ann took over in 1935.

Lewis Morgan was a farmer from South Wales. On October 11th 1935 he hired a train to move all his farm animals (shire horses, Hereford cattle, sheep), farm implements and household furniture from Wales to Brampton Station.

The Morgans farmed at Spratton Grange until Lewis died in 1976, two of their sons, Elwyn and Ieuan, joining them once they had left school.

1954 *Lewis Morgan and his wife Mary Ann.*

1970s *Harvest time on Grange Farm.*
Left to right: ?, Richard Manning, Alwyn Wykes, ? Ronald Buckby, Maurice Barrick, William Anderson, Ray Hammond.

1920s *Sheep shearing in Hall Lane on Gilby's Farm.*

1920s *Potato harvesting.*
Left to right: Susan Adnitt, Richard Adnitt,
Sarah Jane Manning.

1930s *Taking a rest from harvesting.*
Left to right: William Manning, Robert Hammond, Joseph
Manning, Leonard Hayter.

1940s *Ursula Wood (later Mrs Dickens) working as a Land Army girl during the*
Second World War.

1947
Working on the farm.
Left to right: Joseph Manning, Margery Carpenters, Thomas Manning, David Bateman.

1836 *An estate sale at Highgate House. In Lot 8 is a rare mention of the White Horse Inn.*

c1900 *Ann Martin of Spratton making lace at the door of her house. Mrs Martin died in 1918 aged 91.*

Before 1850

Although we know that Spratton was quite important amongst the East Midland villages that produced bobbin lace, there is very little hard evidence available before 1851. This is probably due to the fact that lacemaking was an occupation of the poorer classes, mostly carried out by women at home to supplement the low wages from agricultural work. We do know that sometime after 1827, Mrs Green and Hannah Richardson from Spratton were producing lace for a commercial buyer although there were likely to have been many more. The 1851 census shows 26,670 lacemakers in the three counties of Bedfordshire, Buckinghamshire and Northamptonshire, of which there were 33 recorded as living in Spratton. At this time, the industry was already in decline and the numbers reduced rapidly after that date.

However, we are indebted to Mrs Georgina Roberts (more of whom later) for an account of the lace school in Spratton, which may have been in Yew Tree Lane. In many other villages, girls entered the lace school, which was a commercial institution, at the age of five or six, but in Spratton, "The girls left the day school at the age of eight years and joined the lace school, and here the hours were from 6 a.m. to 6 p.m. in the summer, and from 8 a.m. to 8 p.m. in the winter. Half an hour was allowed for breakfast and for tea, and one hour for dinner, so that there were ten hours for actual work. The girls had to stick ten pins a minute, or six hundred an hour; and if at the end of

the day they were five pins behind, they had to work for another hour. On Saturdays, however, they had a half-holiday, working only to the dinner-hour. They counted to themselves every pin they stuck, and at every fiftieth pin they called out the time, and the girls used to race each other as to who should call out first.

They paid twopence a week (or threepence in winter) for lights, and in return they received the money realised from the sale of the lace they made, and they could earn about sixpence a day. Pay-day was a great event; it came once a month.

In the evenings eighteen girls worked by one tallow candle, value one penny; the 'candle-stool' stood about as high as an ordinary table with four legs. In the middle of this was what was known as the 'pole-board', with six holes in a circle and one in the centre. In the centre hole was a long stick with a socket for the candle at one end and peg-holes through the sides, so that it could be raised or lowered at will. In the other six holes were placed pieces of wood hollowed out like a cup, and into each of these was placed a bottle made of very thin glass filled with water. These bottles acted as strong condensers or lenses, and the eighteen girls sat round the table, three to each bottle, their stools being upon different levels, the highest nearest the bottle, which threw the light down upon the work like a burning-glass. The makers of the best lace would sit nearest the light, and so on in order of merit. In the day-time as many as thirty girls, and sometimes boys, would work in a room about twelve feet square, with two windows, and in the winter they could have no fire for lack of room."

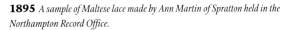

1895 *A sample of Maltese lace made by Ann Martin of Spratton held in the Northampton Record Office.*

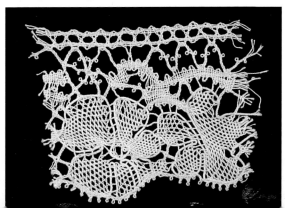

C A MARKHAM (CAM 890)

1895 A sample of Torchon lace made by Hannah Balderson of Spratton. There is no lace known as Northamptonshire lace. The lace being produced in the East Midlands village schools would have been Point Ground or Buckinghamshire Point as it is now known.

Mrs Roberts gathered this account from the recollections of old lacemakers still living in Spratton towards the end of the 19th century. They would have been remembering a time fifty years earlier, so possibly around 1820.

On St. Andrew's Day, the lacemakers at the school in Spratton waited for the mistress to leave the room and then they would lock her out. When she returned, they would sing:

> "Pardon Mistress, Pardon Master,
>   Pardon for a pin;
>   If you won't give a holiday, we
>   Will not let you in."

After a brief display of counterfeited anger, the mistress would give way and the girls had their half holiday.

Attempts to revive the industry

Towards the end of the nineteenth century, attempts were made, initially by local gentry, to prevent hardship by reviving the lace industry, which had then gone into decline. Alice Dryden of the Dryden family at Canons Ashby was one of the more notable ladies who took an interest in lacemaking, but one of the most significant was Mrs Georgina Roberts, who came to Spratton in 1863 as the young bride of Canon Roberts. It is not known where Mrs Roberts learnt to make lace, quite possibly from the older generation of lacemakers in the village, who would be struggling to make a living from this dying industry. By all accounts she was an extremely skilled worker in many types of lace and, once she had learnt the basics, she may have studied other laces from across Europe and mastered the techniques herself. It was unusual for a gentlewoman to pursue lacemaking as a leisure activity and so she describes herself as an 'amateur' to denote the fact that she was not earning a living from her craft.

Mrs Roberts is important for several reasons, not least because she left us the above account of the conditions endured at the lace schools in the early part of the century. She also, with the aid of a subscription, began to buy lace from workers who were suffering hardship due to the decline of the trade, and she re-sold this to her friends. In 1891 it is recorded that Mrs Roberts was responsible for "receiving and buying" lace, which was placed in the depot (in the shop of

c1900 A lacemaker sitting outside her cottage at the bottom of Holdenby Road. (Only one of these cottages is still standing.) Lacemaking was done at home by poor people to supplement the meagre household income. Cottage windows were small and an open fire could easily soil the delicate lacework so, when weather permitted, lacemakers would take their pillows outside to take advantage of the natural light.

Messrs Adnitts), Northampton. Local people will recall that Adnitts was in the premises in The Drapery, now occupied by Debenhams.

An 1891 report on the state of the lace industry, was prepared for the Department of Science and Art by Alan S Cole of the then South Kensington Museum. Having commented on Mrs Roberts' work, Mr Cole went on to say that "at Spratton there are probably some 20 or 25 lace workers, most of them old women, who have been out in domestic service and, having returned to live in the village, add to the home purse by working at their pillows... There are no children at Spratton learning lace making."   Mr Cole visited some of these workers but did not name any of them. Mrs B. remembered "how her sister would get a pattern off the frosted glass of the windows in winter and drar un on to paper and then prick it off on the parchment down for working." Mrs C. was "making some tiny edging lace, of which about four hours a day work would produce 12 inches or a down, the payment for which would not probably exceed twopence." This seemingly tiny amount would no doubt have been a valuable contribution to the weekly income. Mrs E. used to keep a lace school and taught boys as well as girls; sometimes as many as 22 pupils. Mrs F. learnt lacemaking 20 years previously at a lace school in Kisslingbury (sic), where there were three such schools.

Mr Cole also visited the National School in Spratton and spoke to the master and mistress, along with Mrs Roberts and a Miss Langham. He discussed the possibility of introducing pillow lacemaking in the school. He went on to visit four more lacemakers in the village, including Mrs H. who had attended a lace school at Naseby and considered an earning of 6 pence a day to be good. Mrs I. and Mrs J. had both been in service, but had managed to continue to do some lacemaking. After she married, Mrs J. had made a piece of lace to trim a christening cap for her daughter Polly.

An exhibition of needlework and pillow lace was held in St Giles' Church Building, Northampton, on 3rd February, 1891 and was opened by HRH the Duchess of Teck, accompanied by her daughter, May, later to become Queen Mary. By all accounts this exhibition was a great success. No doubt Mrs Roberts would have been involved in the organisation but she also

1910 *Miss Channer's lace school and business at the end of High Street, Spratton. From here she gave lessons and sold lace, as will be seen from the sign outside. It is not known who are the two people standing at the gate.*

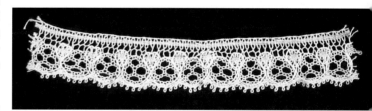

1895 *A sample of Honeycomb and Bud lace made by Mrs Green of Spratton. Spratton appears to have been known for its 'baby' lace—narrow Buckinghamshire edgings used to trim baby clothes. Of course, the lacemakers themselves would not have used or worn lace. Any lace that could have been sold would have gone through the dealers to the local gentry or even to markets in London and would have provided a much needed income for the maker.*

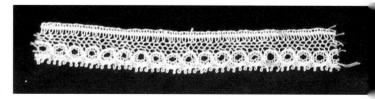

1895 *A sample of One Eyelet lace made by Mary Copson of Spratton.*

exhibited some of her lace in the amateur category along with Miss Langham. Professional workers from Spratton, many of whom received prizes, were Mrs Martin, Mrs C Hitchcock, Mrs Purser, Mrs J Green, Mrs Copson, Mrs W Dunkley and Mrs Maria Dunkley. It was reported in the Spratton Parochial Magazine that £44 worth of lace was sold, "a great boon to many a poor household. It is hoped that it will tend to the improvement of the pillow lace trade, which has unfortunately, of late years, fallen to a low ebb."

It was directly from this exhibition, that the Midland Lace Association, of which Mrs Roberts was a founder member and, for a short time, manager, was formed. The purposes of the organisation were to improve the local manufacture of lace, facilitate sales and provide instruction in lacemaking. Countess Spencer agreed to be President of the Association and many other local gentlewomen served on the committee but Mrs Roberts' lacemaking skills and knowledge of

c1910 *Miss Channer at her lace pillow, surrounded by many beautiful pieces of lace. She was not only an accomplished lacemaker but also understood the industry and the reasons for its decline. Consequently, she was a passionate advocate for technical education.*

techniques would have played a major part in sustaining this dying industry for many more years. The records show that between 1914 and 1923 there were six workers from Spratton supplying the Midland Lace Association, as well as Spratton Lace School, run by Miss Channer.

Georgina Roberts was to continue promoting lacemaking and in 1926, two years before she died, she produced a booklet entitled *Instructions in the Art of Making the Buckingham Pillow Lace*. It has been suggested that the patterns explained in her book were those being produced by the lacemakers in Spratton, but

there is no evidence for this being so. In the introduction to her book, Mrs Roberts reports that in 1894 Countess Spencer requested from her a box of lace on approval to HRH the Duchess of York (later Queen Mary). A variety of patterns made by the Midland Lacemakers was sent and the Duchess chose four. Six dozen of each pattern were ordered, (elsewhere it is reported as 360 yards) and the order was to be completed in one month.

Lacemakers in Spratton and other villages were set to work and the lace was finished in six weeks. Mrs Roberts received a letter from a lady in waiting "expressing Her Royal Highness' satisfaction with it and thanking me for getting it done in so short a time." The lace supplied was used to trim the baby clothes for Prince Edward of York, later Edward VIII.

Canon and Mrs Roberts had several daughters, one of whom was Margaret Roberts. Margaret left Spratton in 1899 on her marriage to Henry Chubb, then curate of Spratton. It is not known if she learnt to make lace with the skill of her mother, but she did study design at the Technical School in Northampton and taught herself to apply this training to the design of new lace

SPRATTON LACE AGENCY.

SPRATTON,
NORTHAMPTON.

Dec. 2nd 1910

Dear Madam,
Thank you for letting me see the lace. I should have no difficulty in both cleaning and mending this lace if you cared for me to do it. It is most beautiful work, I enclose receipt with thanks.
Yours truly
Catherine C. Channer

1910

This letter sent by Miss Channer from the Spratton Lace School indicates that, as well as teaching and selling lace, she also cleaned and repaired it. She would also re-style older pieces of hand-made lace into more fashionable collars of the day.

patterns. She is principally known for her collaboration with Catherine Channer on *Lacemaking in the Midlands. Past and Present.* "This book describes the situation of the local workers and makes an impassioned plea for the Education Committee to have the skills taught in schools." Miss Roberts and Miss Channer were both daughters of members of the clergy. Catherine Channer moved to Ravensthorpe in 1894, when her father became the vicar there. She may have learnt her lace under the guidance of Mrs Roberts but during the 1890s, when she was still in her twenties, she was teaching Valenciennes lace in Spratton and East Haddon, travelling between the villages on bicycle or horseback, with her lace pillow strapped to her saddle. Just before the book was published, Miss Channer travelled to India where she found lacemaking to be "a splendid occupation for jungle life" and taught the skill at the Scots Mission at Kalimpong.

Upon her return to England, Miss Channer worked for the Midland Lace Association and set up a lace school in Spratton. From 1914 until 1930, she moved her business to St Giles Square in Northampton and later to Abington Street and taught at the College of Arts and Crafts in St George's Avenue. There is very little detail about Miss Channer's time in Spratton, or indeed in Northampton, but her contribution to the cause of lacemaking is significant and she is perhaps the single most important early influence on the modern day craft of bobbin lacemaking. Her book *Practical Lacemaking* published in 1928 not only gave instructions for working lace, but provided a new generation of lacemakers with the skills to draft their own patterns and thus keep the craft alive. Catherine Channer moved to Bedford around 1930, where she taught at the Technical Institute. She died in 1949.

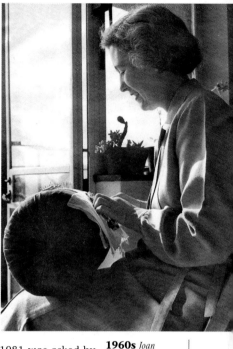

The twentieth century

One of that new generation of lacemakers was Miss B Joan Savage, who moved to Spratton in 1970, to a cottage in the High Street, just a few doors away from Miss Channer's lace school. She was a member of Northampton Embroiderers' Guild and in 1981 was asked by them to produce a gift for Princess Alice, Duchess of Gloucester, on the occasion of her 80th birthday. The wide Torchon lace handkerchief edging took many, many hours to produce and was mounted on fine lawn by Miss Savage herself. She was very proud of her fine needlework and bobbin lace skills and, indeed, of her collection of old bobbins, which had been purchased for pennies when the industry was in total decline. Many of her friends were delighted to receive a Torchon lace bookmark made from her own special pattern and using coloured threads in a very modern and imaginative way.

Athene Frisby

1960s *Joan Savage at her lace pillow before she moved to Spratton. She came to Northampton to study occupational therapy at St Andrew's Hospital and probably her interest in lace came through her work there.*

1981 *The handkerchief made by Joan Savage for Princess Alice, Duchess of Gloucester, for her 80th birthday. The photograph was taken just before the work was completed and shows the bobbins still in place on the pillow.*

Chapter Seven

THE VILLAGE SCHOOL

1919 *Spratton village school when Mr Harry Smith was the schoolmaster. The house on the left is the School House which has now been demolished. The children are smartly dressed and the boys are wearing Eton collars.*

We do not know what sort of building was used as the school in those early days, but in 1847 the main classroom was a thatched barn. There was no heating and no lighting in the buildings until the first few years of the years of the 20th century when lamps and open fires were provided. In 1879 the schoolmaster, Mr Edward Adams protested at temperatures of 38°F in the classroom by sending the pupils home. An architect's report in 1910 commented that the arrangements for admitting fresh air were unsatisfactory, the lighting was defective and the thatched roof was in poor condition. The lavatories were described as offensive and were a great nuisance in the summer as the smells penetrated the school! The Local Education Authority more or less condemned the school buildings and the only remedy was for the governors to appeal to the residents of the village for support and financial help. Over the next few months the necessary money was raised.

By the time school records began in 1866 with the log book of the schoolmaster, Mr James Griffiths, the standard of education had deteriorated from the high hopes of the school's founders. No doubt this was partially due to the amount of absenteeism among the children caused by the importance to parents of the whole family earning extra cash at harvest times.

The school we know today as Spratton Church of England Primary School was founded in 1819 when the local squire, Robert Ramsden of Spratton Hall, endowed a Free School for Girls and Boys and also an Infants' School. Robert Ramsden took a great interest in education and, together with the vicar, the Rev Robert Crowther, and the schoolmaster Mr John R Pridmore, helped to make Spratton more advanced educationally than its neighbours. For many years there were only two teachers: a mistress for the infants and a schoolmaster for the rest of the school.

The curriculum consisted of general subjects as well as *a systematic instruction in the Christian religion so that in accordance with the Trust Deeds there might be given instruction in the Catechism and in the doctrines and principles of the Church of England to all children whose parents desire it.*

c1903 *An early photograph of the children of Spratton village school with the schoolmaster, Mr Harry Smith. The girls are neatly dressed with pinafores and the older boys, as well as Mr Smith, are formally dressed with jackets and collars.*

Children were employed on the farms for harvesting, bird 'frighting', pea and potato picking, gleaning and carrying tea and beer to their working parents. A report of 1847 stated, *As the school lies in the neighbourhood where the utmost apathy exists among parents with regards to education, and is inspected so soon after gleaning which is followed by a village feast, it is not possible to fairly estimate its true worth. The children seem to have everything against them in the way of home influence and the landowners only very feebly support the vicar's self-denying effort on behalf of elementary education. Many of the children had hardly attended once during the last three months and so were not in good discipline.*

For many years schoolmasters George Munton and Edward Adams struggled to keep up the attendance figures which fluctuated wildly from 66 children to 160 according to the time of year. Indifference to education was not the only problem. Scarlet fever, diptheria, whooping cough and epidemics of influenza, mumps and measles in the village kept the children away from school.

c1900 *A school outing for the boys The children have been carefully posed and are dressed smartly with polished boots and warm clothes including their Eton collars.*

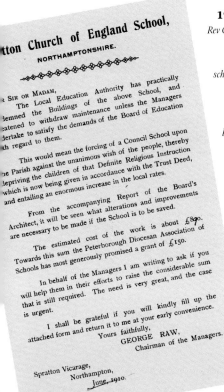

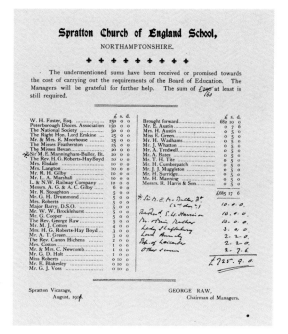

1910 *The vicar, the Rev G Raw, chairman of the managers (governors) of the school, sent out a letter to the whole village asking for help to repair the school buildings. The total cost for the major refurbishment was £820, a very large sum for a small rural community to find.*

OR SIR OR MADAM,
The Local Education Authority has practically ...demned the Buildings of the above School, and ...eatened to withdraw maintenance unless the Managers ...dertake to satisfy the demands of the Board of Education ...th regard to them.

This would mean the forcing of a Council School upon ...he Parish against the unanimous wish of the people, thereby ...depriving the children of that Definite Religious Instruction ...which is now being given in accordance with the Trust Deed, ...and entailing an enormous increase in the local rates.

From the accompanying Report of the Board's Architect, it will be seen what alterations and improvements are necessary to be made if the School is to be saved.

The estimated cost of the work is about £890. Towards this sum the Peterborough Diocesan Association of Schools has most generously promised a grant of £150.

In behalf of the Managers I am writing to ask if you will help them in their efforts to raise the considerable sum that is still required. The need is very great, and the case is urgent.

I shall be grateful if you will kindly fill up the attached form and return it to me at your early convenience.

Yours faithfully,
GEORGE RAW,
Chairman of the Managers.

Spratton Vicarage,
Northampton,
June, 1910.

Spratton Church of England School,

NORTHAMPTONSHIRE.

✛ ✛ ✛ ✛ ✛ ✛ ✛ ✛

The undermentioned sums have been received or promised towards the cost of carrying out the requirements of the Board of Education. The Managers will be grateful for further help. The sum of £200 at least is still required. *160*

	£	s.	d.		£	s.	d.
W. H. Foster, Esq.	250	0	0	Brought forward	682	10	0
Peterborough Dioces. Association	150	0	0	Mr. E. Austin	0	7	6
The National Society	50	0	0	Mrs. H. Austin	0	5	0
The Right Hon. Lord Erskine	25	0	0	Miss E. Green	0	5	0
Mr. & Mrs. F. Moorhouse	25	0	0	Mr. H. Wadhams	0	5	0
The Misses Featherston	25	0	0	Mr. J. Whatton	0	5	0
The Misses Bevan	20	0	0	Mr. A. Tredwell	0	5	0
Sir M. E. Manningham-Buller, Bt.	20	0	0	Mr. A. Bates	0	5	0
The Rev. H.G. Roberts-HayBoyd	10	0	0	Mr. T. H. Tite	0	5	0
Mrs. Elsdale	10	0	0	Mr. H. Cumberpatch	0	5	0
Mrs. Langton	10	0	0	Mr. J. J. Muggleton	0	5	0
Mr. R. H. Gilby	10	0	0	Mr. H. Surridge	0	5	0
Mr. L. A. Marshall	10	0	0	Mr. H. Manning	0	5	0
L. & N.W. Railway Company	10	0	0	Messrs. R. Harris & Son	0	5	0
Messrs. A. G. & A. C. Gilby	6	0	0				
Mr. R. Stoughton	5	0	0		£685	17	6
Mr. G. H. Drummond	5	0	0	*Sir M. E. M. Buller 2d* *(2d don ²)*	10	0	0
Mrs. Roberts	5	0	0	*Richard C.H. Harrison*	10	0	0
Major Barry, D.S.O.	5	0	0	*Mr. Rain Father*	10	0	0
Mr. W. W. Brocklehurst	5	0	0	*Lady Shepherding*	3	0	0
Mr. G. Cooper	5	0	0	*Lord Armsby*	2	2	0
The Rev. George Raw	5	0	0	*Bp. of Leicester*	2	2	0
Mrs. M. J. Cotton	5	0	0	*Other sums*	2	7	6
Mrs. H. G. Roberts-Hay Boyd	3	0	0				
Mr. A. T. Green	3	0	0		£725	9	0
The Rev. Canon Hichens	2	0	0				
Mrs. Cotton	1	0	0				
Mr. & Mrs. C. Newcomb	1	0	0				
Mr. G. D. Holt	1	0	0				
Miss Roberts	0	10	0				
Mr. E. Blakesley	0	10	0				
Mr. G. J. Voss	0	10	0				

Spratton Vicarage,
August, 1911.

GEORGE RAW,
Chairman of Managers.

1911 *The list of subscribers to the restoration of the school buildings is interesting in that Mr W Foster heads the list with a very generous £250, far more than any other benefactor. Although Mr Foster owned Spratton Grange, in 1910 he lived in his family home in Shropshire and rented out the Grange to Mr and Mrs E Moorhouse.*

1900s *May Day at Spratton School when Mr Smith was the school master. The pupils are dressed formally and the photograph composed with care to show the children at their best.*

When Mr Harry Smith became the schoolmaster in 1889 he set about improving the buildings, the discipline of the children and the standard of teaching. In 1894 he was awarded the Langham prize given to the school most satisfactory to the examiners in all respects. In July 1896 Spratton's first County Council scholarship was gained by Harry Blakesley aged 13 years to enable him to go to the Northampton and County Technical School for two years. The first girl from Spratton to win a scholarship was Emily Austin who in September 1896 was able to go to the Northamptonshire County Council School for Domestic Economy. Mr Smith gained the respect of pupils and parents alike and it is interesting to note in the school log books how many young soldiers who had been at the school in their childhood came back from the trenches when on leave in the First World War to talk to him and show him their medals and decorations.

Even the excellent Mr Smith had his problems, however. Village life did not suit some of the teachers, more used to the excitements of the town. One young woman began work on 6th January 1896 and walked out on 24th January owing to the extreme dullness and monotony of life in a village.

In March the teacher appointed to replace her was so incapable and unsuccessful that she had to be dismissed and in April the next teacher appointed refused to come.

Mr Smith retired in 1924 after 35 years teaching in Spratton.

1929 *Caroline Billing was May Queen. In 1930 she became mid-Northants schoolgirl sports champion.*

Mr George L Shaw was appointed to follow Mr Smith and to keep up his high standards. The number of scholarships increased and many pupils went on to university after secondary school. Edgar Eldred, aged 14 years, won a prize in The Times picture tinting competition and the children came third singing at the Mid-Northants Music Festival. School Attendance Officers helped to keep the pupils at school. Parents were fined if their children missed too many sessions. Despite the improvements that had been made to the school buildings, Mr Shaw wrote in his log book on 12th February 1929 that the thermometer showed 32°F in one of the classrooms and the ink in the inkwells was frozen until lunch time.

Mr Shaw encouraged excellence in sport and in 1930 Caroline Billing became Mid-Northants girls' sports champion (tying with one other girl). They shared the cup, each holding it for six months. In 1934 Spratton girls again produced a county champion in Sheila Buswell and the team won the girls' shield. The boys, not to be outdone, won the boys' Shield in 1936.

1934 *the year Spratton Girls' Sports Team won the County Shield. Left to right: Phyllis Cooper, Madge Smith (Wingrove), Mr George Shaw Head Teacher, Sheila Buswell Team Captain with the Shield, Joan Lovell, Leila Buswell.*

During the Second World War many evacuee children arrived from London and needed to be educated. Mr Shaw and his staff devised a system whereby Spratton pupils were taught in the morning and the evacuees were taught by their own teachers in the afternoon. This was reversed on alternate weeks. In 1940 the W I Hall next door was used for the visitors and everyone enjoyed normal all day schooling. By the end of the war 315 evacuee children had passed through Spratton school.

Mr Shaw retired in 1950 after 26 years as Headteacher.

2004 *Mr Darren Sibley, Headteacher of Spratton Church of England Primary School, and some of his pupils being interviewed for Anglia Television during rehearsals for the village play about the churchyard cross and Sir John Swinford. Left to right: Louise Fletcher (apprentice), Anna Smith (2nd apprentice), Amy Hewitt (Lady in waiting), Darren Sibley (Sir John Swinford), Sarah Beecroft (Anglia TV presenter), Gary the cameraman.*

1990 *The winner of the annual village Pancake Race on Shrove Tuesday was Mr Owain Evans, Headteacher of Spratton Church of England Primary School from 1982-1991.*

1996 *Headteacher Mrs Beverly Gascoin (1991 – 2002) with one of her pupils.*

1974 *Headteacher Mr James Courthold (1974-1982) with Gillian Haynes and Connie Wykes.*

Head Teachers

1819	John R Pridmore	1889	Harry Smith
1849	William Taylor	1924	George L Shaw
1851	Benjamin Gander	1950	Thomas Mitchell
1866	James Griffiths	1970	John Wilkinson
1869	Benjamin Brown	1974	James Courthold
1870	George H Munton	1982	Owain Evans
1877	John H Wardale	1991	Beverly Gascoin
1878	Edward Adams	2002	Darren Sibley

65

The Dame's School

This was a small private school in the village which seems to have closed down in 1872. Very little is known about it but on November 11th 1872 Mr George Munton, the schoolmaster of the village school, wrote in his log book, *Had an increased attendance at school, several being admitted owing to the closing of a Dame's School—the only other Elementary School in the village. They were all pretty tolerable dunces, and not much used to any discipline.*

The Dame's School is mentioned again some years later so the actual date of closure is not certain. The school may have been housed in a cottage in Church Road and / or near to the Olde White Horse Inn in the Brixworth Road.

1989 *The children of the primary school gathered together to say goodbye to Hazel Hardy who had been their school meals supervisor for 14 years. Helping them along at the piano was Marianne Oakes.*

1989 *Class 4 with their teacher Mrs Beverly Gascoin.*

1980 *Music making at Spratton primary school. The recorder group hard at work under the direction of Richard York. In the group are Emma Clark, Samantha Matthews, Claire Greenwood, Emma Forsey, Michelle Wykes, Karen George, Tara Hollowell, Sadie Poulton, Sarah Kilsby, Joanne Gowland, Paula Hardwick and Jessica Poulton.*

The present school

In 1952 the school was handed over by the Church of England to Northampton Education Authority and became a voluntary controlled school. Today it is a thriving Church of England primary school taking in children from Spratton and the local area according to parental choice. The school buildings and facilities are greatly improved and there are now four full time teachers and three learning support assistants as well as the Headteacher. The school prides itself on preparing its pupils for life in the 21st century and provides a stimulating and welcoming environment. The children gain confidence and a measure of independence in the happy and well-ordered surroundings and also an understanding and deeper appreciation of our Christian heritage. The academic standards achieved by the children today are well above the national average.

1976 *Group of children from Spratton primary school. Left to right: Charles Murray, Stephen Brown, Ian Pye, Andrew Addleton, Alison Mason, Kirsty Gascoin, Christine Barlow.*
In the background: Alison Jones and Maria Jones.

1995 *Years 3 and 4 with their teacher Margaret Scott (left).*
The school bursar, Elaine Boutle sits on the right.

Chapter Eight

SPRATTON IN WAR TIME

CHRISTMAS & NEW YEAR GREETINGS

1916-17 *A Christmas card sent from the trenches of World War I by Thomas Billing to his family in Spratton. Private Billing served in the Queens Royal West Surrey Regiment.*

The Great War
World War One 1914—1918

The first men from Spratton to go to war, Thomas Horne, Walter Blakesley and Walter Wykes, left in August 1914. The vicar urged the rest of the young men of the village to sign up to fight. In his Parish Magazine November 1914 Rev G Raw wrote, *Their King and Country need the young men of Spratton. May it be theirs in years to come to be able to say, 'We were wanted and we went.'* Fifty seven men responded to the propaganda and joined up. When they came home on leave some went back to the village primary school where they had been pupils to talk to the schoolmaster, Mr Harry Smith. Mr Smith recorded the fact that in 1917 Lieutenant Reeve had just come back from Buckingham Palace where he had received the Military Cross for gallant service from the King. He was given a public reception in Northampton on his return. Lieutenant Reeve had been wounded four times and had also won the Distinguished Conduct Medal for gallantry in action.

Sergeant Frederick Balderson of the Gloucestershire Regiment also went to see Mr Smith at the beginning of October 1917 just before he went back to fight in the trenches. He told him that he had won the Military Medal for bravery in the field. Sadly later that very same month Sergeant Balderson was killed aged 23 years in the 3rd Battle of Ypres. His name is recorded on the Tyne Cot Memorial in Belgium. Sergeant Webb of the 1st Warwickshire Regiment also visited Mr Smith having won the Military Medal and the Distinguished Conduct Medal. Most of the young men from Spratton served in the Army, but three served in the Navy (Archibald Copson, A Horne and Ernest Kench) and one in the newly formed Royal Flying Corps (Lt William B Rhodes-Moorhouse VC).

Battle of Waterloo

General Whichcote lived at Spratton Hall in the 1840s. He served with the British army under the Duke of Wellington and fought in the Battle of Waterloo in 1815 when Napoleon was defeated

Chelsea Pensioners

In 1851 there were three Chelsea Pensioners living in Spratton: John Freeman born 1779, John Ward born 1779 and Joseph Beaumont born 1808. From the ages of the first two men it would seem likely that they fought in the French wars with the Duke of Wellington's army against Napoleon.

South African War 1899 - 1902

Three men from Spratton served in the South African (Boer) War 1899 – 1902. They were Walter Martin, William Manning and Alfred G Gilby of the Buckinghamshire Yeomanry. When Trooper Gilby came home from the war a banquet was held in his honour. The Spratton Brass Band played and there were sports and dancing. Children at the village school were given a half day holiday on 1st March 1900 for the Relief of Ladysmith and another half day on 24th May for the Relief of Mafeking.

1916 *Joseph and Mary-Ann Copson's family. A happy family photograph probably taken in 1916. With five sons and three sons-in-law fighting in the war, this might well have been the last time the family were all together. Happily all the men returned home at the end of the war. Left to right: (Standing) Joseph, a daughter-in-law, Alfred, Archibald (navy), Margaret (a daughter-in-law), Ebenezer, a daughter in law, John. (Sitting): Mabel, Bertha, Joseph, Mary-Ann, Mary-Ann (daughter), Mary Hannah. (Children): Edna (daughter of Mabel), Thomas and Sheila Whitton (children of daughter Mary-Ann).*

Meanwhile back in the village a Voluntary Defence Force was set up with Mr Muggleton from the bakery in charge. Joseph Copson, who had five sons and three sons-in-law fighting in the war, helped with the VDF. Sidney Holt remembered seeing Zeppelins over Northampton when he was a small child. His father fetched a gun and said he was going to shoot them down if they came close. He did not, of course! Spratton House became a hospital and rationing had to be introduced because of submarine warfare. German prisoners of war held at Brixworth helped out on the land, as did some of the farmers' daughters. It was an unusual sight in those days to see women in trousers working on the land and some of the older farmers did not like it. Old Mr Gilby was heard to exclaim, "Don't know what things are coming to—lasses in breeches!"

When the war ended and the young men returned home a splendid 'Welcome Home' party was held and the Spratton Brass Band gave its very last performance at the village peace celebrations.

First World War photographs

Young men going to fight in the Great War were encouraged to have their photographs taken in a professional studio before they left England. Photographs of First World War soldiers in this book all show clearly the studio background and the formal poses arranged by the photographer.

1914-1918 *Private Harry Cook stands against a pleasant background of greenery, flowers and sky in the photographer's studio. He rests his hand on a carved stone pillar and stands smartly looking straight at the camera. He joined first the Norfolk and then the Northamptonshire Regiments. He fought in France and came home safely at the end of the war.*

War Memorial

Under the great cedar tree on the highest point in the churchyard overlooking the Brixworth Road stands a Memorial Cross to the men of the parish who died in the terrible slaughter of the Great War 1914 –1918. It was unveiled on Sunday April 3rd 1921 by General Lord Horne and dedicated by the vicar, the Rev George Raw. The names of 18 young men are inscribed on metal panels. Of the 57 men of Spratton who enlisted in the First World War, the following did not return and are commemorated on the War Memorial.

Private **Herbert C Austin** of the 1st Battalion, Highland Light Infantry, who died of wounds in May 1915 and is buried at Lewisham (Ladywell) Cemetery in London.

Corporal **Frederick Balderson M.M.** of the 14th Battalion, Gloucestershire Regiment who was killed in action aged 23 years in October 1917 at the 3rd Battle of Ypres. His name is on the Tyne Cot Memorial in Belgium which bears the names of almost 35,000 men whose graves are not known. He was the son of John and Julia Balderson and was awarded the Military Medal for bravery in the field.

Private **Thomas Albert Cook** of the 2nd Battalion, Bedfordshire Regiment who was killed in action aged 30 years at Ypres in September 1917. His name is on the Tyne Cot Memorial in Belgium. He was the son of Thomas and Sarah Ann Cook.

Harry Owman Copson of the Royal Engineers who was killed in action in France in October 1917. He was the son of Henry and Mary Ann Copson.

Private **George Manning** of the 1st Battalion, Queen's Own Royal West Kent Regiment, who was killed in action at Vimy Ridge in May 1917. He was the son of John and Sarah Jane Manning and is remembered on the Arras Memorial in France.

Private **Benjamin G Green** of the 7th Battalion, The Queen's (Royal West Surrey Regiment), who was killed in action on the Somme in November 1916. His is buried in the Connaught Cemetery, Thiepval. He lived in First Turn, Spratton, and was the son of Thomas and Hannah Green.

1914 *George Manning of the Queen's Own Royal West Kent Regiment took his family with him to be captured on film before he left to fight in France. His wife sits on an ornate chair in front of a painted open window while his youngest daughter is perched on a table. George himself in uniform stands behind his eldest daughter who looks confidently at the camera. They would have been wearing their best clothes for the occasion. George did not return to Spratton. He was killed at Vimy Ridge in July 1917.*

Private **Walter E Hayter** of the 1st Battalion, Northamptonshire Regiment, who was killed in action aged 21 years in July 1915 and is buried in the Quarry Cemetery, Vermelles, France. He is also remembered in an inscription on the grave of his mother Priscilla in the old Spratton Cemetery on the Brixworth Road.

Lance Corporal **Lewis Horne** of the 8th Battalion, East Yorkshire Regiment, who was killed in action aged 23 years in May 1917 and whose name is inscribed on the Arras Memorial in France. He was the son of Thomas and Emma Horne

Driver **John H Leeson** of the Royal Field Artillery, who was killed in action in October 1918 and is buried at the Communal Cemetery in

1915 George Martin poses smartly with hat, gloves and stick against a studio woodland back-ground with a carved table as a prop. He was sent out to India to fight with the Royal Field Artillery and died of fever after being wounded in 1917.

Valenciennes, France. Having fought in the Battle of Mons, he was awarded the Mons campaign medal. He was the son of Joseph and Martha Leeson.

Private **E Reginald Letts** of the 1st Battalion, Northamptonshire Regiment, who was killed in action in France in May 1915.

Gunner **George A Martin** of the Royal Field Artillery who died of a fever in hospital in October 1917 after being wounded in action in India. He is buried in Karachi Cemetery and is remembered on the Delhi Memorial (India Gate). He was the son of Joseph and Elizabeth Martin.

Private **Arthur Walter Page** of the 5th Battalion, Northamptonshire Regiment, who died in Leicester in July 1915 aged 20 years from wounds received at Ypres. He was buried in the old Spratton Cemetery on the Brixworth Road with full military honours together with his parents Alfred and Sarah Page.

Lieutenant **William Barnard Rhodes-Moorhouse V C** of the Royal Flying Corps who was killed in action over Courtrai on 26th April 1915.

Private **William John Smith** of the 1st Battalion, Northamptonshire Regiment, who died in November 1914 aged 21 years at Ypres. His name is recorded on the Menin Gate at Ypres. He was the son of Elizabeth and Reuben Smith.

Private **Ernest Tite** of the 13th Battalion, Royal Sussex Regiment, who died in April 1918 aged 20 years at Ypres and whose name is recorded on the Tyne Cot Memorial in Belgium. He was the son of Thomas and Charlotte Tite.

Joseph Tyrrell of the Royal Army Service Corps who was killed in action in France.

Private **John Edward Wadhams** of the 6th Bedfordshire Regiment who was killed in action in France in March 1918.

T. Edwin Wadhams of the Machine Gun Corps who was killed in action in France.

Lieutenant W B Rhodes-Moorhouse – First Airman to Receive a Victoria Cross

William Barnard Moorhouse, the elder son of Edward Moorhouse of Spratton Grange, was born on 26 September 1887 and was educated at Harrow and Trinity Hall, Cambridge. He took the name of Rhodes-Moorhouse in 1914 to comply with the terms of his grandfather's will. Before joining the Royal Flying Corps when war was declared he had learned to fly and had become a pioneer in the relatively new world of aviation.

Having been commissioned on 22 August 1914 his first post was in charge of the Royal Flying Corps workshops at South Farnborough. The following March as a Second Lieutenant he joined No 2 Squadron, No 1 Wing at the front and was killed in a bombing raid over the railway junction at Courtrai, France, a month later in April 1915 aged 28 years. He was awarded the Victoria Cross, the highest honour for bravery in the presence of the enemy, and also posthumously promoted to Lieutenant. The first airman to receive the award, he was also entitled to the 1914-1915 Star, the British War Medal and the Victory Medal. His Victoria Cross was sold in 1990 at the RAF Museum, Hendon, and the money used to establish a charitable trust in his memory. His son, Flying Officer W. H. Rhodes-Moorhouse, was

1915 *The BE 2b aircraft used by the Royal Flying Corps at the beginning of the First World War. It was very light, being made of canvas stretched over a wooden frame. William Rhodes-Moorhouse was flying a BE 2b when he won his Victoria Cross.*

killed in the Second World War in the Battle of Britain aged 26 years and was buried by the side of his father in the family home in Dorset.

The London Gazette announced the award of the Victoria Cross on 22nd May 1915 as follows:

1914 *William Rhodes Moorhouse working on his Austro-Daimler motor car in the uniform of Second Lieutenant, Royal Flying Corps.*

To the late W B Rhodes-Moorhouse, Special Reserve, Royal Flying Corps, for most conspicuous bravery on 26th April 1915, in flying to Courtrai and dropping bombs on the railway line near that station. On starting the return journey he was mortally wounded, but

succeeded in flying for 35 miles to his destination, at very low altitude, and reported the successful accomplishment of his object. He has since died of his wounds. This officer was flying a BE 2b.

29th April 1915 from the 'Daily Bulletin'
Details are now to hand of the successful air raid carried out on 26th inst. It is a story of amazing gallantry and heroism and is worthy of special notice. The aviator, 2nd Lieut Rhodes-Moorhouse, left Merville at 3.05 in the afternoon, alone in a biplane, to drop a heavy bomb on the railway junction at Courtrai. Arriving at his destination, he volplaned down to a height of 300 ft. While at this low altitude he was subjected to a tornado of fire from thousands of rifles, machine guns and shell fire. He was severely wounded in the thigh, part of which was shot away, but instead of descending into German lines, where his life might have been saved, and to prevent his machine falling into the hands of the Germans, he turned and made for British lines. To increase his speed he descended a further 200 ft and crossed the German lines at a height of 100 ft only. He was again severely wounded by a bullet which ripped open his abdomen. Instead of landing at Ypres, he flew the whole way back to Merville and made his report. We regret to say that he succumbed to his wounds twenty-four hours later. This would appear worthy to be ranked among the most heroic stories of the world's history.

This was first issued at the special request of the Indian Corps, who had seen him flying back, and 'were so impressed by his astounding courage' that they had asked for further details. It was translated into Hindustani, and afterwards circulated to all our troops.

April 1915 *Informal group of airmen from No 2 Squadron, Royal Flying Corps, at the military base at Merville, France. Second Lieutenant William Rhodes-Moorhouse is sitting with his back to the camera. Despite being fatally wounded, he made his way back to Merville at a very low altitude after his successful raid on the railway junction at Courtrai. He insisted on making his report before having his wounds treated. He died here 24 hours later and was posthumously promoted to Lieutenant.*

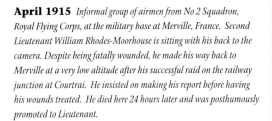

The Second World War 1939—1945

1944
Mabel Balderson served in the WAAF.

Once again the men of Spratton went to fight for their country, this time in all three services: the Army, the Navy and the Air Force. For the first time women played an active part in the war and joined the Auxiliary Territorial Service (ATS), the Women's Auxiliary Air Force (WAAF) and the Women's Royal Naval Service (WRNS). The Women's Land Army arrived to help the farmers and they worked with German and Italian prisoners of war. Children helped in the fields too when they were able. Welfare organisations such as the Women's Voluntary Service were set up, orange juice and cod liver oil were distributed and billets were found for those evacuated from the cities. Stella Gilby was the Billeting Officer for Spratton. Every adult and child over five years was issued with a gas mask. Knitting and needlework groups, such as the one organised by Leila Church, provided comforts for the troops. Charles Gilby was in charge of the Air Raid Patrol (ARP) formed in 1936.

The Army requisitioned Spratton Grange in 1939 and used it at first for housing evacuees from the East End of London. Spratton House was requisitioned in 1940 by the Canadian Light Infantry and later the Medical Corps. Broomhill became a convalescent home for troops. Soldiers stationed at these bases would gather in the local public houses when they were off duty. At *The Chequers* villagers came to know the soldiers well as they all enjoyed themselves singing round the piano.

Spratton hardly suffered at all from bombing during the war. Older villagers remember enemy planes jettisoning bombs left over from a raid on another town. They fell in a field near Brixworth Lane and killed some hens. Some unexploded bombs were found between Spratton and Brixworth and the road was closed for several weeks. People also remember the sound of a flying bomb passing over Spratton later in the war. It came down in Creaton and hit the butcher's shop but no-one was hurt. That evening a dance was being held at the W I Hall with Mr E Copson as the master of ceremonies. Despite his urging people to stay and continue dancing, most people were upset by the sound of the bomb and left to go home to their families. The village was kept awake the night that Coventry was bombed. There was the noise of hundreds of bombers passing overhead as they flew in from the east and the muffled sound of many explosions. The sky was red with light from the city on fire and in the morning the acrid smell of burning was carried into Spratton on the breeze.

A large 'Welcome Home' party was held for the returning soldiers at the end of the war and VE and VJ Days were celebrated with street parties, sports and holidays from school for the children.

1940
George Thomas Manning served in the Northamptonshire regiment.

June 1943 *Broomhill became an annexe to Northampton General Hospital. Some of those wounded in the war came here to convalesce.*

Women's Land Army

By the beginning of the war there was a severe shortage of men to work on Britain's farms. Most had enlisted in the army, but many had left agriculture because of the low wages. It became vital to produce more food crops at home because the German U-boat campaign was preventing food supplies from overseas from reaching our shores.

The government decided to re-form the Women's Land Army (first set up in World War One). By November 1939, 25,000 young women from towns and cities as well as from the countryside had volunteered to work on the land. They wore a uniform of green jumpers, brown trousers and brown felt hats and did many jobs around the farms such as milking, ploughing and bringing in the harvest. The Women's Land Army helped to keep Britain supplied with food during the whole of the war and by the time it was disbanded in 1950 over 90,000 women had taken part in the scheme.

Forty Land Girls were billeted at Brampton House in Chapel Brampton and worked on farms in Spratton and the surrounding area. They played an important part in keeping the country self-sufficient in food.

1939 *A poster issued by the government to persuade women to volunteer to help the war effort.*

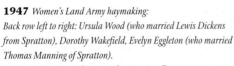

1947 *Women's Land Army haymaking:*
Back row left to right: Ursula Wood (who married Lewis Dickens from Spratton), Dorothy Wakefield, Evelyn Eggleton (who married Thomas Manning of Spratton).
Front row: Patricia Robertson, Christine Lavell.

1947 *Women's Land Army. Even though the war was over, there were still food shortages and rationing of food was in place. The girls from the Land Army worked on until 1950 when the organisation was disbanded. These girls, Margaret Richardson, Evelyn Eggleton and their friend, were part of a pruning group, sent round to various farms to prune trees in the orchards.*

1941 - 42 The Home Guard outside Gilby's Farm

Back row: Harold (Timmy) Manning, George Billingham, Mr Davis (from Blagdens shippers and exporters temporarily at Broomhill), Mr Biggar (from Blagdens), Donald Pateman, Michael Cook, Lewis Dickens.

Second row from back: Bard Leeson, Cyril Perkins, Peter/Ronald Broughton, Francis Butcher, Pop Dickens, James Griffin, Ronald Bell, Frederick Chapman.

Second row from front: Lance Corporal Alfred (Mac) Macaness, Corporal Percy Richardson, Sergeant Ebenezer Copson, Archibald Copson, Major Flint (Commanding Officer), 1st Lieutenant Ernest Bryant (Second in Command), Sergeant Walter Wykes, Lance Corporal William Adams, Alfred Smith.

Front row: Ronald Pateman, Robert Manning, George Hayter, Charles Manning, Leonard Wykes.

The Home Guard

The Home Guard was formed in 1940 when there was a real danger of invasion. They were needed to delay the enemy for long enough for the regular army to come and take over. Volunteers for the Home Guard were those men who were either too old or too young to enlist or those in 'reserved' occupations (jobs vital to the war effort). To begin with their weapons were whatever they could lay their hands on, but later they were issued with more conventional rifles. By the end of June 1940 over one million men had volunteered for the Home Guard.

In Spratton it was the task of the Home Guard to patrol the village and to guard important spots from Creaton to Brixworth. Among those who volunteered were veterans of the 1914-18 war (Archibald and Ebenezer Copson), shopkeepers (Percy Richardson) and landlords (Ernest Bryant of *The Fir Tree*). Major Flint (formerly of 20th Lancashire Fusiliers) was in command with the landlord of *The Fir Tree* as his Second in Command. Apparently Major Flint stored bombs in the outbuildings of his headquarters and home 'Rathgar' (now the Old White Horse Inn). Despite his assurance that the detonators were missing, his neighbours were not amused! The Home Guard was disbanded in December 1945.

The War Memorial

The War Memorial was erected in the churchyard in 1921 and dedicated to the memory of the men who died in the First World War. At a later date six further names were added to the memory of those who fell in the Second Great War 1939 – 1945

The following men who died in the Second World War are named on the War Memorial:

Private **Richard Charles Adnitt** of the 6th Battalion, Northamptonshire Regiment who was killed in action in November 1942 aged 24 years. He is buried in a Commonwealth War Grave in the old Spratton Cemetery on the Brixworth Road and was the son of Richard and Susan Adnitt.

Corporal **Thomas Henry Buckby** of the 2nd Northamptonshire Yeomanry, Royal Armoured Corps, who died in July 1944 aged 24 years in Normandy. His name is recorded on the Bayeux Memorial, France. He was the son of Harry and Kate Buckby.

1939 Richard Adnitt served in the Northamptonshire Regiment and was killed in 1942. In this photograph he would seem to be wearing his best friend's RAF uniform.

Private **Walter Roy Copson** of the 5/7th Battalion, the Gordon Highlanders, who died aged 21 years in January 1945 in Normandy. His name is recorded on the Bayeux Memorial, France. He was the son of Mrs F Copson.

Trooper **Stanley Higgs** of the 4th Regiment, Reconnaissance Corps, Royal Armoured Corps, who died in November 1944 aged 26 years in Italy, during the advance from Rimini to Forli across flooded rivers in atrocious weather. He is buried in the Cesena War Cemetery, Italy and was the son of William and Mary Higgs.

Sergeant **John George Manning** of the 8th King's Royal Irish Hussars, Royal Armoured Corps, who died aged 25 years in April 1945 in the Rhineland, Germany. He was the son of George and Eva Manning and is buried in the Rheinberg War Cemetery, Germany.

Private **Charles Richard Herbert Wing** of the 2nd Battalion, Royal Norfolk Regiment, who died in May 1940 aged 29 years during the evacuation of the British Army from Dunkirk. He is buried in the Dunkirk Town Cemetery, France.

1992 The War Memorial in St Andrew's churchyard Spratton, commemorating those who died in two world wars, was unveiled on 3rd April 1921 by General Lord Horne GCB, KCMG, and dedicated by the vicar, the Rev George Raw. The Celtic cross of Hornton stone was made by the firm of J G Pullen.

TRANSPORT

1929 *Spratton Station with a Renown 4-4-0 LNW 1954 LMS 5121 Galatea, rebuilt from 'Alfred the Great' October 1924.*
The London to Birmingham railway had been built in 1838 by-passing Northampton. On 16th February 1859 a branch line (London and North Western Railway) was opened from Northampton to Market Harborough, stopping at Brampton, Brixworth and Lamport. It was an 18 mile single line track and two trains each way ran daily. In 1864 LNWR opened a new station where the line crossed the Spratton to Brixworth road, with four trains each way stopping daily. Because of increased usage another track was built and the double track line was opened on 4th August 1879. On 23rd May 1949 Spratton Station was closed completely and the last train ever to run – a 'passenger special' – ran on 15th August 1981.

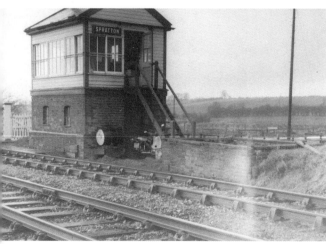

1973 *Spratton signal box and level crossing.*

1974 *A close up of Spratton signal box with the level crossing gates in the background.*

1950s *Spratton signal box with William Parrot of Brixworth who was the signalman during the 1950s and 1960s.*

Station masters and signalmen at Spratton Station

1871	Isaac Hicks (Station master)
1874	Abraham Matthews (Station master)
1878	John Crabb (Station master)
1893	John Crabb (Station master)
1910	Mr Mayse (Station master)
1950s	William Parrot (Signalman)
1960s	William Parrot (Signalman)
1970s	George Mitton (Signalman) and Colin Green (Signalman)

1934 *A 4-wheel contraption (velocipede) made by Peter Saul (on the left) with his uncle Ted Mitchley, passing Gordon Sharp, taking a census on the Welford Road by the bridge close to the Boughton cold store.*

16th August 1981

The last train ever to run from Northampton to Market Harborough approaching Spratton level crossing. This was a passenger train making a special run to mark the final closing of the line. Spratton station had been closed in May 1949.

c1908 *William Moorhouse riding a penny farthing bicycle at Spratton Grange.*

1910 *William Moorhouse, the son of Edward Moorhouse of Spratton Grange, working at the wheel of his Peugeot motor car. He was passionately interested in motor cars and motor cycles. In 1906 he drove a 6 h.p. Riley and a 5 h.p. Humber. In 1908 he owned a Fiat named Linda after his fiancee. Villagers' parents remember him racing round the country lanes in his cars, sometimes carrying children in the back 'to add weight'. The mechanic working on the engine is almost certainly Jack Tookey.*

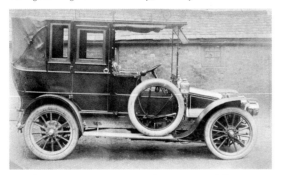

In 1915 *Mr Wood ran a taxi service from Spratton with this new motor car, a Renault Landaulette.*

1930s *Albert Branson standing by Dragon Fly, one of three buses owned by Jack Smith and operated from a depot in Teeton Road, Creaton.*

1912 *William Moorhouse and his wife, Linda, driving near Chapel Brampton. The photograph was taken from the car they were overtaking.*

1914 *William Rhodes-Moorhouse seated in the cockpit of his aircraft just before he joined the Royal Flying Corps.*

The Aeroplane

William Moorhouse (1887 – 1915), a wealthy young man from Spratton Grange, was extremely interested in the engines of motor cycles and motor cars and soon became skilled in racing both. He was fascinated by the new aeroplanes and pooled his resources with another more experienced aviator, James Radley, to produce a version of the Bleriot XI aircraft – the Radley-Moorhouse monoplane. He took flying lessons at Huntingdon and caused a sensation when, on returning from Huntingdon to Spratton, he landed his plane on Northampton Racecourse. He had navigated by following a road route he knew and had kept warm by wearing seven shirts and an overcoat! He posed for photographs, spoke to a journalist and then took off for home in Spratton. The Northampton Daily Echo reporter who had rushed out to the Racecourse asked him if he had been flying long. Moorhouse replied, "No: about a

week. This is my first cross-country flight. I have only been up before on the machine on our ground at Huntingdon where we are quite prepared to teach you. Nerves? No. I haven't any."

He was granted his Royal Aero Club Certificate on 17th October 1911 and the same day he flew to Northampton to collect some shoes from Messrs. Barratts. These he delivered to Hendon – the first parcel post by air. He visited America where he won a considerable amount of prize money in air races.

He married in July 1912 and marked this by flying with his new wife and a journalist from an airfield in France to England. They completed the 130 mile air flight by crash landing in Kent. No one was hurt, however, and

1912 *William Moorhouse in the cockpit of his Radley-Moorhouse monoplane with his mechanics steadying the very light aircraft and helping him to take off.*

1912 *The Radley-Moorhouse monoplane piloted by William Moorhouse taking off from Northampton Racecourse. The sight was so unusual that crowds gathered to watch.*

Moorhouse had achieved the record of being the first pilot to cross the channel with two passengers.

No doubt this experience on her honeymoon alarmed his wife, and he gave up flying for two years. When war was declared he immediately joined the brand new Royal Flying Corps and was posted to South Farnborough to be in charge of the RFC workshops there. In March 1915 he joined No 2 Squadron at the front and was killed in April 1915 while returning from a bombing raid on the railway junction at Courtai in France. He was awarded the Victoria Cross posthumously for this act of 'conspicuous bravery'.

1912 *William Moorhouse (standing centre) is posing with his friends and mechanics in front of one of the early aeroplanes in which he learned to fly at Huntingdon. Second on the left is Charles Branson, the farm manager at Broomhill at the time.*
The photograph looks as if it could have been an advertising stunt as the very visible poster placed in front is advertising Marshall Bottled Ales, in particular Oatmeal Stout. The brewery was based in Huntingdon.

Chapter Ten
WEDDINGS

6th October 1916 *The wedding of Arthur Dickens of Brixworth and Evelyn Taylor of Spratton. Arthur worked at the ironstone pits in Scaldwell and Evelyn worked at the King's Head. After their marriage they lived in Manor Road. At the time of their wedding Arthur was serving in the 5th Northamptonshire Regiment (Pioneers) in France and went on to fight in the Battle of the Somme. It is interesting to note that because of the restrictions of war time the bride did not wear a long white dress and she did not carry a bouquet of flowers. She wears a corsage of flowers on her dress instead. From the formal background it can be seen that the photograph was taken in a photographer's studio as were many photos of soldiers at the time.*

1920 *at Home Farm. The wedding of Charles and Eleanor Payne. Edward (Teddy) Wykes of Home Farm is standing on the right. This formal, carefully posed photograph is taken outside Home Farm with the ladies wearing the fashionable shorter hemlines of the 1920s. They are all three carrying large bouquets of flowers and wearing flowers in their headdresses as well. Their pale stockings and shoes with curved heels are clearly shown as are the pretty short sleeves and gloves of the bridesmaids.*

Early 1930s *The wedding of Harold Eldred and Elizabeth Byrne. The bride's headdress is similar to those worn in the 1920s wedding on the previous page and large bouquets of flowers are still in fashion. The dresses, however, are made of softer, more flowing fabric and the bridesmaid's floral print with its fluted sleeves and hemline is typical of the fashions of the 1930s. Hemlines are longer than in the 1920s but the shoes are similar. Harold was a haulage contractor who worked with his father's building firm and Elizabeth was in service. They lived first in Brixworth Road and then in the High Street. The wedding photograph, taken at 5 Holdenby Road shows from left to right: Joseph Eldred, Herbert Eldred, Harold Eldred, Elizabeth Byrne, Phyllis Branson, William Byrne (best man and brother of the bride), Rose Eldred.*

Phyllis Branson lived at Spratton Lodge with her sister, Ann, and mother, Florence (nee Martin daughter of lacemaker Mrs Ann Martin). Her father was Charles Branson, the farm manager at Broomhill. Phyllis married Edgar Eldred shortly afterwards and their daughter, Mary, married Dick Spearman, who has been very involved with the Football Club.

15th January 1938 *The wedding of Leslie Green and Caroline Billing. Leslie was a carpenter by trade and served in the Military Police in the Second World War. Caroline (known as 'Cass') was mid-Northants schoolgirl Sports Champion in 1930 and later worked in Spratton Post Office. Both her mother and her grandmother were born in Spratton. The ladies wear simple floral headdresses and, while the bridesmaids carry very large bouquets of carnations, the bride carries an elegant spray of lilies. The full length dresses are made of stiffer fabric than those of the wedding pictured above and are decorated with appliqued flowers. The gentlemen wear formal suits with sprays of heather in their buttonholes. Left to right: Joseph Billing (bride's brother), Rita Wykes, Leslie Green, Caroline Billing, Margaret Billing (bride's sister), Thomas Billing (bride's father).*

1944 *The wedding of Peter Chapman and Kathleen Saul. Peter served in REME during the Second World War and then owned Heap's Garage in Guilsborough after the war. Kathleen worked for her family in Sauls Butcher's shop in Spratton. The wedding photograph shows four young people serving in the military forces in the war. Because of shortages and rationing, the bridal party would have had to save up a large number of 'clothing coupons' to be able to purchase the bride's and bridesmaids' dresses. The bridesmaids hold large formal posies and are wearing fingerless gloves, while the bride carries a spray of lilies and some lucky horseshoes given to her by friends and relatives. All the ladies in the photograph are wearing hats. Back row left to right: 1 ? Peter Saul (brother of the bride), Kathleen Saul (Peter's wife), 4 ? William Saul, Frank Saul (bride's father). Front row: 1 ? 2 ? Bridesmaid Doris, Peter Chapman, Kathleen Saul, Bridesmaid, Cecile Saul. Pageboy, Richard Gilby.*

1940 *Wedding of Edward Hayter and Constance Cory at Spratton Church. The family are dressed warmly for a winter wedding and of the five attendants the bride has chosen no less than three children. The pageboy, in a velvet suit and frilled shirt, looks rather cold and the girls, wearing short dresses and gloves, are carrying large bouquets. The bride carries a large bouquet of deep coloured flowers and some lucky horseshoes. She has a floral headdress and a long, swirling net veil. The photograph has been taken outside 26 High Street.*

Left to right standing: Frank Hayter, Nellie Hayter, Jim Cawley, Edward Hayter, Constance Hayter, John Cory, Miss Jeffs.

Front row: Polly Hayter, Derek Hayter, Maureen Cory, Miss Jeffs (younger sister), Emma Cory.

30th July 1949 *The wedding of Thomas Manning of Spratton and Evelyn Eggleton from London. Thomas was groom and gardener to the Chief Constable, Angus Ferguson, who lived at Spratton Manor, and during the Second World War he served with the Northamptonshire Regiment in the military police. Evelyn was in the Women's Land Army based at Chapel Brampton. The formally posed photograph shows a clearly delighted bride and groom almost hidden by the bride's large bouquet of dark coloured flowers. They are holding the popular lucky wooden spoon and horseshoes. The ladies' dresses contain much more fabric than those during the war years, indicating perhaps that times were getting easier. The bride especially has a full flowing skirt and a beautiful long train. The bridesmaids' dresses all seem to be different styles and once again they are wearing fingerless long gloves. Left to right: Jack Manning (Best Man), Margaret Adams, Ann Manning, Thomas Manning, Evelyn Eggleton, Dolly Blore, Frank Eggleton (bride's brother).*

16th December 1950 *The wedding of Lewis Dickens from Spratton and Ursula Wood from Ireland. Lewis worked on a farm during the Second World War and Ursula was in the Land Army which is how they met. After the war Lewis worked for the Northamptonshire Water Board at Pitsford. The wedding took place on a cold December day just before Christmas with the snow lying picturesquely on the ground. The vicar (not in this photograph) wore his Wellington boots for the photographs! The ladies are wearing full length dresses with plenty of fabric in the skirts and carrying very large bouquets. The bride is wearing a full length lace dress. All the ladies in the photograph are wearing hats and the bridesmaids have long, elbow length gloves.*

1960s *The wedding of Richard Gilby and Lesley Berringer. Richard is the eldest son of Charles Gilby (of Gilby's farm) and was the manager of a farm in the Rushden area. He is the pageboy at Peter and Kathleen Chapman's wedding on page 84. The bride is wearing an elegant, long sleeved dress in a rich silk fabric and has chosen to hold a prayer book rather than a bouquet. The bridegroom wears a formal morning suit with a white flower in his buttonhole. The photograph shows the couple getting into their car after the marriage service.*

1952 *The wedding of Denis Eaton and Irene Bannister. Denis worked in a shoe factory in Northampton. In the photograph, taken outside the church door, the bridegroom holds gloves and the bride carries a dramatic bouquet of red roses and a lucky horseshoe. She is holding up the long train of her dress to protect it from the wet ground. It looks as if their wedding day was blessed with rain! In 1988 Irene Eaton made a large donation towards the installation of a sixth bell in St Andrew's Church in memory of her father, Harry Bannister. She is pictured with the bell in Chapter 3.*

1952 *The wedding of Elwyn Morgan and Gwen Turland. Elwyn and his brother Ieuan farmed with their father Lewis at Grange Farm when they left school. Gwen Turland's father was a butcher at Creaton and Edna, her stepmother, was Headteacher at Creaton School.*
Left to right: Lewis Morgan, Mary Ann Morgan, Pam Turland, Elwyn Morgan, Gwen Turland, Ieuan Morgan, Edna Turland, Sidney Turland. Small bridesmaid: Elaine Morgan.

1961 *The wedding of Terry Hardwick and Ivy Cattell. The bridegroom was a member of the Spratton Football team in the 1960s and his friends have all come, in their football kit, to wish him well. The bride wears a very fashionable short wedding dress and carries a prayer book and a small posy of flowers.*
Standing: Graham Billingham, George Costello, Tom Horner, Terry Hardwick and his wife, Frank Copson (small head), John Eldred, Bob Tite, Roy Mason, Harry Thomas.
Kneeling: Pete Horne, Harry Copson, John Wykes, George Smith.

1979 *The wedding of Christopher Saul and Lesley Le Cornu. Christopher works in the family Butcher's shop which he now owns and Lesley was a teacher. They live in Brixworth Road in Spratton. The photograph shows the bride and groom with their parents. Peter and Kathleen Saul are on the left and Mr and Mrs Le Cornu are on the right. The bride holds a much smaller bouquet than previous brides and she is wearing a graceful, long sleeved lace dress with a full train.*

Chapter Eleven

MAY DAYS

May Day Traditions

It has been the custom for centuries to celebrate 1st May as the arrival of spring. Houses were traditionally decorated with blossoms and groups of young people paraded round the streets, collecting money. Even as far back as mediaeval times fund-raising activities were associated with the May Games. Maypole dancing was very popular and although it was banned at one time by the Puritans, this pleasurable activity was revived in the late seventeenth century and maypoles were raised in villages all over the country. The dancing involved a complicated process of weaving and unweaving coloured ribbons held by the dancers.

In Spratton May Day celebrations over the years seem to have mainly involved children, who danced round maypoles, gathered flowers, made garlands and paraded them round the streets asking for money. On May 1st in 1872 the Headteacher at the village school, Mr George Munton, wrote in his log book, *Children mostly gone exhibiting May Garlands for pence, so no regular school.* On May Day in 1877 he complained, *Only 34 at school this morning of whom 8 only were girls—the rest of the girls, with most of the little boys, having gone Maying, parading the village with a bunch of flowers on a stick to collect halfpence.* A few years later, however, the teachers seem to have decided that everyone should be able to enjoy the ancient custom of celebrating the arrival of spring and a holiday was given to the children on May Day. A May Day tea was provided and they all enjoyed May Day games.

The custom of electing a May Queen seems to have started in Victorian times and here in Spratton we know from photographic evidence that May Queen parades were held every year for much of the twentieth century. Collections were made at first to pay for the children's tea, but in the 1950s the Merry Comrades, a charitable organisation, made collections on May Day for charity.

1928 May Day in Spratton *The traditional May Day celebrations included the May Queen and her attendants walking through the village with flowers. In 1928 Betty Williams was chosen as the May Queen. Standing left to right: William Tarrant, Florence Horne, Nora Manning, Wyn Griffin, Winifred Higgs, Hilda Nutt, Joyce Copson, Ronald Bounds.*
Sitting or kneeling: Audrey Churchill, Caroline Billing, Eleanor Hayter, Betty Williams the May Queen, Joyce Burrows, Joan Page, Leila Buswell.

1932 May Day *In 1932 Mary Attwood was the May Queen. Among her attendants were Gwendoline Higgs, Sheila Buswell, Madge Smith, Dorothy Payne, Margaret Billing, Gertrude Crane and Jean Frisby. Among the small girls were Moira Copson, Christine Manning, Gladys Horne and Enid Horne. Sitting are Dolly Cook and Rachel Copson. The young boy on the right is Anthony Buswell. Part of the celebrations each year involved dancing round the maypole and many people in the village would come out to watch. In this picture a group of mothers accompanies the procession.*

1938 May Day *with Mary Buckby as the May Queen.*
From the late 1890s May Day festivities included giving the children a treat with tea, games and sports. What were the boys doing while the girls were dressing up and having tea?
1 ? 2 Grace Moss 3 ? 4 Louisa Jane Frisby 5 ? 6 Emily Taylor 7 Melba Copson 8 Sis Wykes 9 Joyce Copson 10 May Queen Mary Buckby 11 Thelma Copson 12 Audrey Wykes 13 Moira Copson 14 ? 15 Mary Wykes 16 Mavis Wilkes 17 Sheila Taylor 18 Delia Balderson 19 Evelyn Moss 20 Doreen Roberts 21 Ann Dickens 22 Thelma Harris 23 Joan Hider 24 Doris Manning 25 Barbara Buckby 26 Bet Horne 27 Beryl Tarpley 28 Doreen Phillips 29 Barbara Broughton 30 Doreen Buckby 31 Olive Cattell.

1930s May Day

The procession walked through the streets of Spratton and paused to have numerous photographs taken. Here the maypole has been erected by the cob wall on the corner of Church Road with Holly House, Spratton House and the Shieling in the background. Some of those in the photograph are Millicent Wykes, Hector Manning, Florence Balderson, Phyllis Balderson, Leonard Hayter, Mrs Wooding, Anthony Wykes and Josephine Phillips.

A lovely photograph of a 1930s May Queen, Jane Sharpe, with her little attendants taken in the grounds of Creaton hospital. Some of the proceeds of the fundraising on May Day went to the hospital. In the 1920s and 1930s the flowers for the Queen and her attendants were provided by the head gardeners of the big houses in the village.

Late 1940s May Day

with Selena Dickens as the May Queen.

Left to right: Shirley Wing, Brenda Wykes, Jill Wright, Selena Dickens (May Queen), Ivy Cattell (her wedding photograph is on page 87), ?, Denise Roach, Margaret Chillingworth, Glenda Fitzsimons.

May Days and the Merry Comrades

The Merry Comrades was an organisation that raised money for local hospitals and children's homes. In Spratton they held fund-raising whist-drives, coffee mornings and jumble sales and very successful May Day celebrations during the 1950s. The festivities would last all day, beginning with the crowning of the May Queen in the playground of the village school. After some maypole dancing the May Queen and her attendants would travel in style on the back of a land-rover to the bigger houses and farms on the outskirts of the village. The older boys would carry the maypole and all the dancers would follow. The maypole was an elaborate affair with two sets of ribbons. The younger children danced on the inside of the circle while the older ones did the more elaborate dances on the outside of the circle. After

dancing, refreshments would be served and then, on to the next house. Sometimes the maypole was taken to Creaton Hospital and set up for the patients and staff to watch the dancing. The children presented a bouquet of flowers to the matron at the beginning of the proceedings.

Twenty years later in the 1970s the children of these Merry Comrades reformed the group and continued to organise May Day celebrations. Sue Matthews, the leader of the Merry Comrades in Spratton, remembers that in the 1970s the maypole was much simpler than it had been previously, now having only one set of ribbons. At the first practice 30 children were eager to dance and they all scrambled to catch hold of one of the 12 ribbons. It was then realised that no-one knew the dances and only one child had actually seen a maypole dance. A book from the library and an adult with patience managed to get them ready for May Day.

1957 May Day organised by the Merry Comrades with Ann Churchill as the May Queen.
Back row: Michael Griffin, Gillian Weston, Josephine Burgoine, Marlene Buckby, Diana Weston, John Walmsley.
Middle row: Norman Wykes, Beryl Matthews, Frances Manning, Ann Churchill (May Queen), ?, Jane Attwood.
Front row: Sheila Manning, Barbara Matthews, Caroline Gibbs, Susan Pateman.

1959 May Day organised by the Merry Comrades *at Creaton Hospital grounds. The maypole in this picture has two sets of ribbons. The younger children dance on the inside while the older girls are on the outside.*
Left to right: 1. Mrs Alice Pateman, who ran Merry Comrades 2. Carol Saul 3. Sandra Griffin 4. Christine Sharp 5. Jane Attwood 6. Annette Wykes 7. Cynthia Goss 8. Glynis Jones 9. William Pateman 10. Norman Wykes 11. Patricia Matthews 12. Pauline Martin 13. Beryl Matthews 14. Carol Pateman 15. Caroline Gibbs 16. Irene Wykes 17. Christine Wykes.

1960 May Day *with Margaret Phillips as the May Queen.*
Mrs Winifred Wykes (carrying the crown), Margaret Phillips (May Queen), with Angela Burgoine and Gillian Wykes holding her train. At the back are Wendy Horne and Christine Wykes The May Queen is walking out to be crowned.

1983 May Day and the Merry Comrades

More than 60 children took part in May Day 1983. The day began in the WI Hall with stalls attracting many visitors. The crowning of 7 year old Charlotte Hunt as May Queen was followed by maypole dancing.

Left to right: 1. Nicola Townsend 2. Jeni Wiltshire 3. Shelley Bates 4. Rebecca Oneil 5. Alex Hewes. 6. Mrs Cozzolino, deputy head of the primary school who crowned the May Queen 7. Christopher Matthews 8. Sue Matthews, the Merry Comrades leader who organised the event 9. Maria Costello 10. Lisa Wright 11. Bridget Clark 12. Geoffrey Simons 13. Mandy Wright 14. Sinade Oneil 15. Neil Simons 16. Charlotte Hunt, the May Queen 17. Tina Costello, Lady-in-Waiting 18. Claire Osborne 19. Kirsty Craig 20. Vicky Lyons 21. Vanessa Blowfield 22. Kate Langford 23. Tania Blowfield.

An extract from the Spratton Parish Magazine June 1911

May Day: The children perambulated the village with their May garlands, singing May Day songs and collecting subscriptions towards their tea which took place at the School on May 6th.

The whole of the arrangements were in the capable hands of Mrs Roberts, who, with a willing band of lady helpers, provided an excellent tea to which 150 children sat down and did ample justice. This was followed by games and songs, and the giving of an orange and a bag of sweets to every child at the close.

From beginning to end the festivities were most successful, and the children thoroughly appreciated the great kindness of Mrs Roberts and her helpers for all that they had done for them. Financially, things were well managed. The children collected £2 11s 9d, and the treat cost £2 10s 10d, leaving a balance of elevenpence on the right side.

Chapter Twelve

ROYAL CELEBRATIONS

Queen Victoria's Jubilee
June 21st 1887

At first it was planned to give the children a half day's holiday from school to celebrate the Jubilee Day of Her Majesty's reign but there was so much rejoicing to plan that the festivities had to be postponed until June 23rd. As the programme was to commence at 8 o' clock in the morning and the events were to last all day, a whole day's holiday was given to scholars and teachers.

Queen Victoria's Diamond Jubilee
June 22nd 1897

Everyone was given a day's holiday and tea, sports and bonfires were organised in Spratton. On the village green an oak tree was planted by Lord Erskine. It was rumoured that a gold sovereign had been planted under the tree. The Sparrow Club made a presentation of seats to be placed around the village.

May 6th 1935 Silver Jubilee of King George V

The vicar, the Rev George Raw, has left behind his record of the day. "As in every other part of the Empire, Spratton showed its affection for and loyalty to the King with great thankfulness, rejoicing and enthusiasm. From early morn till midnight our celebrations were carried on, and everything passed off without the slightest hitch."

Street parties were held in various places in Spratton.. Those present at the street party in the High St:

1. Elizabeth Adams (nee Manning) 2. Sarah Jane Manning 3. Charles Manning (son of May) 4. George Manning, 5. Frances Horne, 6. May Manning (George's wife), 7. Arthur Branson, 8. Mary Branson, 9. Mrs Thomas Wykes 10. Mr Fowell 11. Harry Martin 12. Jean Fowell 13. Christine Manning (daughter of May) 14. Kate Martin 15. Doll Wykes 16. Myra Wykes 17. Reginald Branson 18. Ruth Wykes 19. Evelyn Moss 20. Mrs Fowell 21. Sylvia Moss (sister of Evelyn, now Gammage) 22. Olive May Manning 23. Daisy Copson (nee Wykes) 24. Grace Moss (mother of Evelyn and Sylvia).

May 6th 1935 Silver Jubilee of King George V

Another street party was held in Manor Road outside The Chequers. Those present were:

1. Peter Clegg, 2. Lou Horne, 3. Joy Smith, 4. Doll Phillips, 5. Pam Phillips, 6. Mrs Ashley Bates, 7. Gladys Harris, 8. Thomas Harris, 9. Nell Cook, 10. Frank Cook, 11. Bertha Manning, 12. Louise Payne, 13. George Shaw, 14. Rev. George Raw, 15. Fred Tucker, 16. Millie Cattell, 17. Mary Horne, 18. Molly Wingrove, 19. Madge Buckby, 20. Renee Bannister, 21. Gertrude Bannister, 22. Eric Moss, 23. Harry Bannister, 24. Harry Cook, 25. Betty Wilkes, 26. Mavis Wilkes, 27. Bert Wilkes, 28. Betty Horne, 29. Derek Wykes, 30. Cora Wykes, 31. Cynthia Wright, 32. Winifred Wykes, 33. Jenny Horne, 34. Alan Wykes, 35. Mrs Hudson, 36. Lizzie Muggleton, 37. Sheila Burgoine, 38. Jean Roche, 39. Winifred Griffin.

**Coronation of King Edward VII
June 26th-27th 1902**

The children had two whole days' holiday from school, the church bells rang out and the whole village celebrated the coronation of Queen Victoria's son.

**Coronation of King George V
June 19th – 23rd 1911**

The vicar, the Rev George Raw, wrote in the Parish Magazine, The church bells were rung at 5 in the morning and again later on. There was a celebration of Holy Communion at 8 in the morning and a special service at 11. The rest of the day was given up to feasting and rejoicing and at 10 in the evening the bonfire was lit. The celebrations were organised by various committees around the village.

ROYAL CELEBRATIONS

May 12th 1937 Coronation of King George VI

Taken in front of the School House, demolished in the 1950s when the school was extended.

Back row left to right: Edith Cheyney, Kathleen Saul, Rose Bowers, Gladys Harris with Thelma Harris, Bill Cattell, Louise Payne, John Tarrant, Frank Saul, Peter Saul.

Front row: Mary Ann Higgs, Eva Payne, Thomas Harris, Louisa Frisby, Edward (Teddy) Wykes, Kate Bell, Mrs George Payne, Cecile Saul, Violet Pateman.

May 12th 1937 Coronation of King George VI

Taken in the High Street.

1. Nellie Hayter, 2. Mabel Balderson, 3. Rita Wykes, 4. George Hayter, 5. Bobby Manning, 6. Joan Martin , 7. Grace Wykes, 8. Ronald Pateman, 9.?, 10. Barbara Buckby, 11. Joan Hider, 12. Phyllis Balderson, 13. Donald Pateman, 14. Nellie Wykes, 15. Clarice Wykes, 16. Frank Horne, 17. Jack Billing, 18. Alfred Horne, 19. Anthony Wykes, 20. Margaret Horne, 21. Thelma Copson, 22. Inez Moss, 23. Olive Cattell, 24. Derek Hayter, 25.?, 26. Philip Martin, 27. William Manning, 28. Percy Pateman, 29. Leonard Hayter, 30.Thomas Buckby, 31. Margaret Anderson, 32. Marlene Wykes, 33. Delia Balderson, 34. Richard Anderson, 35. Leonard Anderson, 36. Alwyn Wykes, 37. Frank Hayter.

1953 *The Coronation tea party in Charles Gilby's barn on 2nd June 1953.*

2nd June 1953
Coronation of Queen Elizabeth II

This was the first coronation of a monarch to be televised. Since very few homes had sets at that time, Mr Jupp provided a television in Charles Gilby's barn so that those who wished could see the ceremony. Afterwards a celebration tea party was held in Mr Gilby's barn.

Another party was held in a marquee at Sandhills. Unfortunately because of the rain, the sports had to take place at a later date. Both these parties were organised by committees and people donated to a fund to pay for them.

A third party was organised by the Women's Institute, mainly for children and for older folk, but also to cater for anyone not attending either of the other parties. Tea was provided and the children had a fancy dress parade as well as games.

2nd June 1953 *Some of the villagers pose for a commemorative photograph on Coronation Day. The day was extremely wet over the whole country and the Queen's procession in London was soaked. as were the crowds watching. People in this photo are wearing Wellington boots and standing in puddles.*
Back row left to right: H Roach, Jack Walmsley, Tot Bott, Pop Dickens, Neville Frisby, Charles Gilby, Mary Branson, Lewis Dickens.
Front row: Michael Cook, Nell Cook, Eva Payne, Dorothy Payne, Gran Dickens, Mary Manning, Leslie Green, George Eales, Richard Manning,
Richard Darling.

Programme

9.00 a.m.	Breaking of Flag
9.30 a.m.	Church Service
10.30 a.m.	Fancy Dress Parade for Children
11–1 p.m.	Children's Sports
12 noon	Mid-Day Snacks for all the Children up to 15 Years
1 p.m.	Luncheon for Adults 1 p.m to 2 p.m. ; at Mr. Gilby's, Hall Lane Field. Times and Personnel notified before June 2nd
1–3 p.m.	Children's Sports
3 p.m.	Tea for All Children up to 15 years
3.30 p.m. (approx)	Presentation of Souvenirs
4 p.m.	Sports for Adults. Tug-of-War Egg and Spoon Race Sack Race Thread the Needle Wheelbarrow Race, Etc. Competition—Old Folks
5 p.m.	Snacks for All
5.30 p.m.	Sports for Ages 15-21. 100 Yards Obstacle Race High Jump, Etc.
6 p.m.–Dusk	Sports for All
	Sports Prizes ⎰ Presentation 8 o'clock Fancy Dress ⎱ By Mr. R. Darling, President Other Amusements—Time Permitting
Dusk	Lighting of Bonfire Firework Display

Dancing—on lawn of Spratton Hall by kind permission of Mr. K. C. Hunter

Television—All Day at the late Mrs. A. Gilby's House

Prizes for Best Decorated House Presented at 3.30 p.m. BY VICE-PRESIDENT

★

"GOD SAVE THE QUEEN"

BAR OPEN ... ITTED HOURS

2nd June 1953

Official programme of events to celebrate the coronation of Queen Elizabeth II in Spratton.

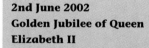

2nd June 1953 *Women's Institute Coronation celebrations - Children's Fancy Dress.*

Back row: Cynthia Hunt, Jill Puttnam, Judith Wright.

Front row: Carol Saul, John Hunt, Belinda Puttnam, Chris Saul, Wendy Haynes.

2nd June 2002
Golden Jubilee of Queen Elizabeth II

The Parish Council marked the occasion by giving every household in Spratton a commemorative glass paperweight

2nd June 1977 Silver Jubilee of Queen Elizabeth II *saw more fancy dress in Spratton, this time in the playground of the primary school. Roger Gascoin wears the naval uniform and Mrs Gardham and Mrs Buckby are among the others in the photograph.*

Chapter Thirteen

VILLAGE SOCIETIES AND EVENTS

Spratton Brass Band

A brass band was formed in Spratton at the end of the 19th century by Mr Thompson and Levi Richardson. Money to buy the expensive instruments was raised by whist-drives, bazaars and fetes. After a particularly successful bazaar held in one of George Cooper's fields in 1890 the Band wrote in the Parish Magazine that they wanted to express *their warmest thanks to all those who on this and other occasions have so kindly assisted them in clearing off the heavy debt upon their instruments.*

Although they were enthusiastic music makers, their playing to start with was not always of the best as the Vicar gently suggested in 1891 after a concert given by the Band for the benefit of widows in the parish. *The attendance was large .... and the Band acquitted themselves very well in four pieces, showing by their execution that they continue to improve, and bearing out the promise to which their* earlier efforts had already given rise. They must have improved with practice because later, under their conductor Levi Richardson, they won second prize at the Village Contest for Brass Bands held at Ravensthorpe.

The village enjoyed their music and they played for many different festive occasions. One such event was the party held to celebrate the return of Richard Gilby's son, Alfred, from the South African (Boer) War in 1901. The Brass Band played on Hospital Sunday each August when they marched round the village collecting for local hospitals.

Many of the bandsmen left the village to fight in the 1914-1918 war, and the last time they all played together was in 1918 for the peace celebrations under their conductor, William Richardson, son of Levi Richardson and church organist for about 36 years.

1904 Spratton Brass Band *(one of the oldest photographs in Spratton Local History Society's archive).*

Back row standing left to right: 1. William Richardson, aged 23, shoemaker, became conductor of the Brass Band after his father 2. Martin Litchfield, aged 36, farmer 3. Levi Richardson, aged 45, shoemaker, one of the founders of the Band and its conductor 4. John Higgs, aged 53, shoemaker 5. Joseph Copson Jnr, aged 15 years 6. Frank Copson, aged 22, carpenter 7. Alfred Copson, aged 25, bootmaker.

Front row seated: 8. Edward Austin, aged 32, carpenter 9. Joseph Copson, aged 49, slipper manufacturer 10. George Payne, aged 30, mason's labourer.

Spratton Fire Brigade

Another early photograph shows the men who were called on when a fire broke out in the village or surrounding locality. Their fire engine, 'a one horse manual', was kept in a shed next to the house at the junction of Church Lane and Yew Tree Lane. The shed is still in existence, but is now a garage.

In September 1911 they were called out urgently at 1.42 pm to a fire at Cank Farm in Brampton. The men responded very quickly and they left Spratton within eight minutes of the call. Having arrived at the fire at 2.04 pm they set to work dousing the flames. It was another hour before the Fire Brigade from Northampton arrived and both groups of men worked hard all afternoon. At 6.00 pm the Northampton men left and half an hour later fire broke out again in the hayricks and barleyricks. Spratton Fire Brigade (15 men) was kept busy all night before the fire was finally put out.

September 1911 Spratton Fire Brigade

Back row left to right: 1. Edward Austin, aged 39, carpenter 2. William Richardson, aged 30, shoemaker 3. John T Manning, aged 34, carrier 4. George Voss, aged 41, bootmaker 5. Ashley Bates, aged 39, bootmaker 6. Henry Cheney, aged 51, bricklayer 7. Albert Green, aged 44, corn and hay merchant, superintendent of the Spratton Fire Brigade.

Front row: 8. Police Constable Jones 9. John Higgs, aged 60, shoemaker 10. George Taylor, aged 41, shoe finisher 11. Samuel Blundell, aged 46, blacksmith 12. George Dunkley, aged 49, bootmaker 13. Henry Surridge, aged 58, master sweep 14. William Higgs, aged 27, shoemaker 15. Levi Richardson, aged 52, shoemaker and captain of the Spratton Fire Brigade.

1930s Men's Outing

Left to right: ?, ?, William (Nebby) Cattell, Ron Bounds, Bus driver, Billy Leeson, Archibald Squires (landlord of The Kings Head) Tom Manning, George Wogan, Joe Billing, Dick Manning, 'Peggy' Martin, Bert Buckby, Phil Emery, Teddy Wykes, Ron Martin, John Matthews, Charlie Wilkes, Reg Tarrant, Tom Cooper, Bill Dickens, Les Crane, Dick Adnitt, Charlie ('Tunk') Copson, George Hayter, Frank Copson Phil Wykes.

1946 Village Fete at Spratton Hall

The organising committee for the first village fete after the war taken in the gardens of Spratton Hall.
Back row left to right: Bob Balderson, George Eales, Hector Wykes, 'Jimmy Riddle' (not from Spratton), Jack Attwood, Jim Griffin, George Anderson, William Cattell.
Front row: Mabel Balderson, Lily Hunt, Maisie Mather, Polly Martin, Sheila Ashley, Ruth Wykes.

Spratton Merry Comrades

The Merry Comrades was a charitable organisation set up in 1908 by the local weekly newspaper The Mercury and Herald. Children formed groups to raise money for local hospitals, special schools and homes. Those children who raised £1 or more would become a captain for that year and be invited to the pantomime at the Royal Theatre, Northampton. They were given a badge which they wore with great pride and sometimes a long row of these could be seen displayed on a strip of felt. If the money was raised without help the child became a star captain and had a different badge. In the early years star captains had their photographs taken on stage but as the Merry Comrades grew in size this became impractical and had to be discontinued.

Each year the newspaper held an Easter and Christmas Bazaar at the Drill Hall or Guildhall in Northampton. A large raffle took place and different branches had stalls. There was great activity in the village leading up to one of these events, with much knitting, sewing, cake making and bric-a-brac collecting going on. The whole village contributed.

Besides the official bazaars, Spratton Merry Comrades organised many fund-raising events themselves. Whist-drives, coffee mornings, jumble sales were all successful as were the May Day celebrations held in the 1950s. (See Chapter 11)

In the 1970s the group was re-formed and many of the new members were children of former Merry Comrades. During the school holidays rehearsals were held for a summer 'pantomime' to be held in the W I Hall before school restarted. The plays were often adapted by the children as they went along to incorporate local people. One year it coincided with relatives holidaying in the village from Canada, America and Australia. One of the older boys made programmes and sold them round the village. The children were often invited to attend the presentation of gifts from the Merry Comrades to local hospitals. In 1977 nearly £200 had been raised in Spratton. In order to reach the full amount a mother was persuaded to have a coffee morning and concert in her house the week before Christmas. In the end a little more than the required amount was raised and the children decided to donate the money to the Spratton Ward at the Princess Marina Hospital. The Merry Comrades were invited to go along to a Christmas party at the ward and entertain the adults living there.

One year a sponsored Litter Collection was held during Keep Spratton Tidy week. The children were sponsored at so much an ounce. At the weigh in the judges were surprised that the litter bags contained not only pieces of paper but also bottles and even a tin of paint. They were assured they had been found under a hedge!

Another event that really showed the generosity and support people had for the Merry Comrades was the annual Egg Collection. This was a very old custom in the village when eggs had been collected by the church to take

1970s

The Merry Comrades and the Pantomime Horse. A play performed in the W I Hall for local charities.

1. Tara Hollowell, 2. Samantha Hammond, 3. Aidan Greenwood, 4. Emma Clark, 5. Anthony Osborne, 6.? 7. Edward Blencowe, 8. Kevin Osborne, 9. Darryl Hinds, 10. Victoria French, 11. Claire Greenwood, 12. Abigail Hunt, 13. Sarah Kilsby, 14. Samantha Matthews , 15. Alex Hewes, 16. Emma Fawcey, 17. Sam Hewes, 18. Martin Bates 19. Sarah Hinds, 20. Tracey Willbank, 21. Libby Roberts, 22. Alison Wiltshire, 23. Ruth Clewitt, 24. Bridget Clark, 25. Charlotte Day, 26. Matthew Hunt, 27. Jeni Wiltshire, 28. Christopher Matthews, 29. Peter Hammond. In the horse: Anne and Roger Miller.

1984 *The Merry Comrades on May Day*

1. James Green, 2.?, 3. Peter Hammond, 4. Tim Dorran, 5. Nicola Townsend, 6. Rev Brian Lee, 7.?, 8. Lisa Wright, 9. June Roberts, 10. Abigail Hunt, 11. Vanessa Blowfield, 12. Christopher Matthews, 13. Sinade Oneil, 14. Maria Costello, 15. Sally Blencowe, 16. Claire Warden, 17. Emma Garle, 18. Mandy Wright.

to people living in the Workhouse in Brixworth. The custom was revived during the Second World War and was still being held by the Merry Comrades in the 1970s. Members would collect eggs from friends, relatives and neighbours and then send them to the local hospital at Creaton. The children were told to go only to people in their own street, but the word soon went round about who was being especially generous and some children knew who kept chickens. One chicken keeper was heard to mutter, "The Merry Comrades are a bit too merry," but was still very generous with his eggs. No one went away empty handed.

By 1988 times had changed and the Merry Comrades was disbanded. Since the start in 1908, over £130,500 had been raised by the children of Northamptonshire.

Most hospital televisions displayed a Merry Comrades brass plate. The first hospital radio system at the Northampton General Hospital was donated by the children. The members at the time wrote their name in a book that was on display at the hospital for many years. Other gifts ranged from scoring cards for a pensioner group to a minibus for the disabled presented in Silver Jubilee Year 1962. When the Merry Comrades finally closed, the residue funds of £9,000 were presented to Northampton General Hospital to refurbish a room to be used for training and seminars. It was named after the leader of the Merry Comrades, Doris Walding ('Auntie Doris'). A fitting tribute to a special organisation.

Sue Matthews

The Women's Institute

The Women's Institute in Spratton was formed in 1923 under the Chairmanship of Lady Erskine from Spratton Hall. They held their meetings at first in the primary school hall but it was felt that they needed a hall of their own and enquiries were made about purchasing some land. Alfred Gilby helped Lady Erskine, Lady Manningham-Buller from Broomhill and Miss Mildred Bevan from Spratton House to purchase The White House in School Road and some adjoining land. The White House was sold and the piece of land was handed in Trust to the Women's Institute, with the three ladies being the first Trustees.

A men's committee was formed to give help and advice on the building of a hall and the W I members set about fund raising. Dances, concerts and whist drives were held and several ladies in the village deposited sums of money, free of interest, with the bank to cover the building costs. The hall was built and the money paid off in a very short time. The opening ceremony of the new Women's Institute Hall was held in August 1928.

Not only has the Hall been used by the Women's Institute for their monthly meetings and events, but also other groups in the village have held their dances, film shows, whist drives and concerts there. During the Second World War it was used to provide meals for Canadian soldiers and also the Home Guard. Evacuee children had their school lessons and their meals there.

The Women's Institute has brought together the women of Spratton for educational purposes as well as social ones. In the past they provided speakers and demonstrations on country and home crafts, folk dancing, drama, cookery and many other topics and arranged classes with the help of the local education authority.

In January 1949 Mrs Alfred Gilby entertained all the members past and present at a Twenty First Birthday celebration, with all the original members sitting at the top table. In 1993 the W I members celebrated their

1930s Women's Institute Outing

Back row standing left to right: Bertha Manning, Irene Lee, Marjorie Brown, Edith Tarrant, Louise Buckby, Isabel Wykes.
Middle row seated: Elizabeth Wykes, Mary Morgan, Annie Wadhams, Emma Tarrant, Emily Tucker.
Front row on grass: Mary Ann Higgs, Daisy Copson, Mrs Pearson (George Cooper's housekeeper), Elizabeth Martin..

70th Birthday with a fine dinner and the cutting of a cake.

There was a membership of 50-60 in the early 1950s but times have changed and the women of Spratton lead very different lives from those of days gone by and membership has decreased. The Hall is showing its age and needs refurbishment. The committee of

the Women's Institute has decided to make a gift of their Hall to the village. A Village Hall Committee has been formed and the old W I Hall is being refurbished thanks to a very generous donation from one of the W I members. From 2005 it will have a new lease of life as Spratton Village Hall.

1983 Members of the Women's Institute standing outside their Hall in their 60th Anniversary year.
Left to right at back: Mary Holt, Gwen Jeffrey, Mary Langdell, Edith Amos.
Front: Goldie Cochrane, Ada Berridge, Hazel Hardy, Mrs Hughes, Sheila Bradshaw, Irene Eaton, Marian Cooper, Kathleen Saul, Marion Brown, Mary Favell, Evelyn Manning.

21st May 1993 *70th Birthday celebrations of the Women's Institute*
Back row left to right: Pauline Boyes, P Harris, J Francis, Diane Hitchcock, Susan Tait
Front row: Mrs Torbette, Mrs Dickens, Frances Roseblade, Margaret Mayhew, Kathleen Saul, Mrs Aisthorpe.

Spratton Parish Council

Parish Councils were formed, as a result of a government initiative, at the end of the 19th century. The first meeting of the Spratton Parish Council took place on 14th November 1894 when Christopher Markham was elected Chairman. Lord Erskine was Vice Chairman, and Northamptonshire Union Bank Ltd became the treasurers.

The members of the new Parish Council threw themselves energetically into an inspection of the wells in the village – these being Batemans (which was very dirty), Mannings, Pound, Austins, Mains (near the school and in a very bad condition) and Tassells which had had an unauthorised pump erected above it. Some £32 of work was carried out by Messrs Cheney Bros and George Kimbell to put the wells to rights.

They inspected the Parish Chest which included bibles, books of Common Prayer, Overseers books (1731-1836), Constables books (1783-1835), Overseers of Highways books (1775-1823), Churchwardens account books (1751-1810), and old Rate books. The Fire Brigade was one of their responsibilities. Rules for the operation and conduct of the brigade were drawn up requiring 15 firemen to be elected and three practices to be held a year.

The Parish Council was also responsible for electing the Constables whose job was to keep law and order in the village. Constables served for one year and were usually elected on a rotation basis from among the better-off members of the

Early Chairmen of Spratton Parish Council

Christopher Markham	1894
Lord Erskine	1896
Richard H Gilby	1904
Albert Green	1905
Harry Smith	1907
Sir Mervyn Manningham-Buller	1910
George Cooper	1914
Harry Smith	1925
Arthur C Gilby	1928
Joseph Copson	1932
Rev George Raw	1935
George Cooper	1937
Charles Gilby	1945

The first minute book ends at 1948

Wednesday 28th October 2004

A party given for Councillor Bill Wood's 80th birthday at the King's Head was attended by past councillors and chairmen of Spratton Parish Council. Bill has been a Parish Councillor for 42 years. Wishing Bill well are past Chairmen Chris Prior Jones, Chris Saul, David Cooke, John Hawtin, Lynne Fowkes, Peter Hunt, Bill Wood (seated), Barry Frenchman (present Chair), Jim Mallard.

community. This voluntary position was mediaeval in origin and was replaced by the police force during the 19th century. In 1896 Peter Leamark, Francis Dixon, Levi Richardson and Henry Riddle were elected as probably the last Constables in Spratton. Other responsibilities included footpaths, management of the local sewage bed, local roads, and cemeteries.

Today the ten members of the Parish Council meet every month and organise their work into four committees: Finance, Planning, Highways and Cemeteries & Open Spaces. They also represent the Parish in the local area and push forward new initiatives and developments to benefit all ages in the community. They particularly encourage village organisations and businesses. Any member of the village is very welcome to attend the public sessions which form part of the Parish Council's monthly meetings.

Town and Charity Land

The Charity Commissioners of 1676 recorded that a number of people living in Spratton (John Pearson, Arthur Goodday, Thomas Hill are among those named) had left either money or land to help those less fortunate than themselves and also to help the community in general. All the money was used to purchase land which was let as allotments and the income used for the charitable purposes stipulated by the original benefactors. It was given 1) to help the poor and destitute with coal, clothing and other necessities, with linen, bedding, tools, food, medical and other aid in sickness; 2) to repair the highways and bridges of Spratton; 3) to maintain and repair the fabric of the church'; 4) to put out as apprentices poor children of the Town of Spratton; 5) to provide prizes for deserving children attending the Public Elementary School and funds to encourage their attendance at school.

Today the charity administers several acres of agricultural land on the west side of the A5199 between the Brixworth Road and Smith Street. It was intended that the land should be used for allotments but now only 20 plots are in use and the rest of the land is leased for grazing. The annual income of the charity is about £3,000 and this is distributed in the following way: 1) One quarter of the income to maintain and repair the church fabric. 2) One quarter for the relief of those in need – usually the trustees make grants in time of bereavement. 3) One quarter for grants towards further education so that

students can purchase books, and grants to the school, scouts, guides and youth club. 4) One quarter for local projects which have included the Recreation Ground, the play group and the Women's Institute.

Recreation Field

After the last crop had been harvested from the 7.4 acre field on Smith Street in the autumn of 1951 Audrey Gaywood Darling sold the field for £750 to a new group of trustees headed up by the Spratton Parish Council. The field was to be 'held in trust as a public ground' and the rules then set up were later incorporated into the Spratton Recreation Field Charity.

The first management committee covered a wide cross section of Spratton village organisations including: the Rev Dennis Pettit for the primary school, G Riddle for the Parish Council, J and G Coleman for the Football Club, Jim Griffin and Bob Tite for the Cricket Club, Mrs Burgoine and Mrs Branson for the Women's Institute and Mr Hunter for Spratton Hall School. In addition there were representatives from the Baptist Chapel, the Roman Catholic Church and the British Legion.

The whole village set to work to raise funds for the new Recreation Field and the money was quickly put to use for football, cricket and tennis. In 1977 the Football Club, with support from the Parish Council, purchased a surplus wooden hospital ward and transported it to the Recreation Field to form the basis of a social club for the village. This was finally completed in 1983.

More recently, some young people in the village under the guidance of Terry Broughton decided to fund raise for a new skateboard park. After much hard work the cash was forthcoming and the skateboard park was opened in 2004.

Youth Club

A Youth Club was formed in 1994 to cater for the young people in the village between the ages of 11 and 16 years. Weekly or fortnightly informal get-togethers are held in the Sports and Social Club where they play pool and darts, listen to music or play on the play station.

Sometimes more organised evenings are held, such as bingo or quizzes, bowling or ice skating outings. Approximately 20 young people attend the Youth Club.

Scouts

In 1940 John Vincent, a dairyman and milkman, started the first Spratton Scouts with 30 boys from Spratton and surrounding villages. The troop only lasted two years and closed in 1942. Mick Capon and Martin Lloyd restarted the Scouts in 1976 and for a number of years produced a Scout and Guide show called 'Three Cheers' which was performed in the W I Hall. The Group closed in 1983 when both leaders left and continued their scouting in Northampton.

1996 *The opening of the Scout Hut (The John Allen Memorial Hall) by Sir John Lowther on 28th April 1996.*

1982 *The Scouts taking part in the annual village clean up. Third left is David Sutch, far right Darren Walmsley with brother Andrew third from the right in the skip.*

Graham Smith, who had moved to the village and was Scout Leader at Brixworth, transferred to Spratton and restarted the Scouts in March 1985, with meetings taking place in the village school. During this time a significant part of the group's history took place – the purchase of the old Catholic Church in Yew Tree Lane. It became known that the building was going to be sold under sealed bid and, after many bids via Chris Saul's shop fax machine, the Scouts were eventually successful in purchasing the building and land to the rear. After much fund raising, generous donations and a great deal of hard work the Headquarters was officially opened by Sir John Lowther, who was president of Northamptonshire Scouts on Sunday 28th April 1996.

Graham left the Group in 1999 to become District Commissioner and Ian Brett took over the Leadership. Following Ian's resignation in May 2004, Graham returned as Scout Leader. Also in May 2004 girls were admitted into the Scout section for the first time in the Group's history. Four girls were invested.

After a long absence without a Group Scout leader, Andrew Elliott accepted the invitation and took up the position in 2002. The Group at present has 66 young people, 10 leaders and 8 instructors with a good supportive Group Executive Committee chaired by Chris Saul.

Cubs

The Cub pack under the leadership of Mick Wright started in 1975 and has been continually running since then. It has had many Leaders, one being Alistair Brooker who is now Brixworth Assistant District Commissioner for Cubs. Sue

1982 *Scouts, Cubs, Guides and Brownies who took part in the 1982 Gang Show, 'Three Cheers'.*

1937 *Sheila Church at the Guides camp in Castle Ashby. She was the first Captain of the Spratton Girl Guides.*

Reader is still helping at cubs after 22 years and is the longest serving leader at the Group. At present the Cubs are under the leadership of Jenny Woodford from Chapel Brampton.

Beavers

In April 1995 Kat Smith started the Beaver section of the Scout Group who still meet in the village school. They have always had a full membership with a waiting list of young people wanting to join.

Guides

Sheila Church (now Mrs Bradshaw) was persuaded by the local District Commissioner to set up a Girl Guides company in Spratton in 1936. Thirty three girls joined and many younger ones wanted to be included as there was no Brownies group at the time. The Guides met on Mondays from 6 – 7pm at the village school and later at Broomhill. Sheila Church was the Captain and Rebecca Belben, the granddaughter of Mrs Foster of Spratton Grange, her Lieutenant. Mrs Church held a bridge party at Broomhill to raise funds to buy uniforms and these were kept and passed on from one girl to another.

The girls went on small expeditions and hiked through fields near Holdenby. They went blackberrying, cooked sausages and eggs in the open air and were taught to swim at the public baths in Northampton. They were grouped in patrols named after birds such as Kingfisher and Robin.

When war was declared in 1939 Sheila Church joined the services as a FANY (First Aid Nursing Yeomanry) driver with the 6th Anti Aircraft Division and the Guides company was closed down. It has re-opened and now has 14 Guides.

Brownies

There was a Brownie pack in Spratton in the 1950s with Mrs Freeburger as the leader. They wore a dark brown dress with a brown belt topped off with a beret. The village school was their meeting place.

1985 *Brownies. The leaders are Christine Osborne (sitting left) and Cherill Hammond (back right).*

Linda Fletcher remembers some of the topics the Brownies were taught, such as how to wash up after a meal and how to lay a table. She went to Margaret Wykes, house in Sandhills for her tests. Linda and Viv Hemp are the 2004 leaders of the 24 Brownies in the pack.

1985 *Guides. The leaders Jan Hewes and Beverly Gascoin stand in the back row.*

Early 1950s Outing to Wannock Gardens, Polegate, Sussex

Back row left to right: Sidney Smith, Winifred Smith, Jenny Dunkley, Mary Branson, Albert Branson, George Dunkley, Florence Favell, Carrie Hart, Harriett Cattell, Brian Smith, Brian Sargeant.

Third row: Bob Balderson, Betty Furnell, Margaret Branson, Ann Horne, Margaret Leeson, Bard Leeson, Albert Horne, Mary Buckby, Dorothy Manning, Tom Horne.

Second row: Doris Phillips, Edith Tarrant, Mary Tarrant, Margaret Adams, Elizabeth Adams, Isabel Hider, Nora Wykes, Kate Buckby, Kate Horne.

Front row: Gladys Balderson, Polly Hayter, Winifred Horne, Lilian Wykes, Dick Buckby, Phoebe Buckby, Doll Phillips, Bert Phillips with John Phillips, Ivy Novak, Margaret Phillips.

1950s Baptist Chapel Outing

Left to right: Richard Berrill, Mrs Richard Berrill, Mrs Sprague, Mrs Somerfield, Florence Favell, Edith Tarrant, Mrs Reynolds, Cora Wykes, Mrs Harry Wykes, Mary Tarrant, Eva Manning, Mary Ann Higgs, Ethel Wykes, Miss King, Winifred Horne, Rhoda Eldred, Elizabeth Billing.

1954 Dance Club Christmas Party
Back row left to right: Mabel Eales, Cicely Tarrant,
Alice Copson, Margaret Wykes, Jean Winston.
Front row: Ruth Wykes, Mary Manning.

The annual pancake race
Each year on Shrove Tuesday a pancake race is held in Spratton. Above: In 1992 The winner was Darren Sibley, a teacher at the Church of England
Primary School.
Right: 1991 PC Barry Vine and Chris Saul.

1923 *The Spratton and Teeton Conservative Club*
was built on the site of the old pinafore factory that
employed many people in Spratton from 1899. The
building shown in the photograph was bought from
Miss Mildred Bevan in 1916 by Sir Mervyn
Manningham-Buller, Arthur Gilby and George Cooper
with their own funds. They became the first Trustees of
the club. The members raised enough money to
purchase the club in 1923. To begin with, only those
who joined the Conservative Party could become
members, but by the time the club was sold and the
building demolished at the end of the 1990s it had
become a village social club. A private house now
stands on the site.

Spratton Garden Club

In 1979 John Tarrant and John Matthews, both keen allotment gardeners, realised that they would be able to buy seeds and other garden supplies at a better rate if they formed a garden club. Dick Manning, Frank Copson, Dick Wykes, Edgar Eldred and Bert Buckby were keen to come in as founder members and Bill Wood was invited to join as treasurer to keep the books in order. Thus was born the 'Spratton and Teeton Conservative Club Allotment and Garden Section'. Its original objective, to act as a co-operative for the allotment holders, was funded by a very successful weekly football card lottery which soon had significant funds in the bank for the club.   The co-operative acquired a hut for the allotments in 1981 with garden supplies available to members, purchased seeds and seed potatoes for sale to members, and organised the piping of water to the allotments. This was completed in 1985 after much discussion with Spratton Town and Charity Land owners of the allotment land.

A natural outlet for keen growers of vegetables and flowers was the establishment of an annual produce show, first held in 1980 and subsequently as a joint show with the Women's Institute. An annual outing to a large garden was introduced in the 1980s and an annual plant bring-and-buy coffee evening was established in 1989.

By the mid 1990s the use of the allotments had reduced considerably, and the hut was sold off. Interest in the produce show was in decline, and after having to be cancelled twice – in 1995 due to exceptionally dry weather, and in 1997 as it clashed with the funeral of Diana, Princess of Wales – it never re-emerged.

Seed ordering, however, has remained an exceedingly popular facility for members with £800 or so of seeds being obtained annually by Len Hayter at a very competitive rate.   Clearly, though, with the decline of allotment activity and the demise of the produce show, the club had to find a new direction.   It now has two or three outings a year, retained the popular coffee evening, and introduced three or four evening talks a year.   With a membership of around 100 people, the club has moved from its allotment roots to a successful club for garden lovers.

1991 *Len Hayter with his prize-winning onions at the 1991 Garden Club and W I Produce Show. Len was secretary of the club from 1993 to 2002.*

1991 *Tom and Kathleen Smith, members of the Garden Club for 15 years.*

1991 *Gordon Pickles examines the winning flower arrangements at the 1991 annual produce show.*

1989 *Painting and Flower Exhibition Local artists exhibited their work in church together with a flower display in the summer of 1989.*

1989 *At the Painting and Flower Exhibition the flower displays were based on themes. The arrangement below commemorates the boot and shoe trade.*

May 2004 Mediaeval Flower Display

The flower arrangement in the chancel used old English flowers with connections with Our Lady. All the flowers used were grown in England in the 14th century.

The arrangement was made by Joan Shaw.

May 2004 Mediaeval Flower Display

The flower display in the window above the Twigden plaque celebrates the American connection in Spratton Church with old English flowers in red, white and blue and the American flag. The arrangement was made by Frances Roseblade.

8th May 1995 50th Anniversary of VE Day

Spratton celebrated the 50th anniversary of VE Day (Victory in Europe 1945) in style with bands, processions, fancy dress parades, traditional games, pony rides and war-time type food.

1995 Three World War Two veterans pose for the camera beside a historic military vehicle. Left to right: Bob Balderson,who served in the Middle East and Greece in the Royal Army Service Corps; Jack Attwood, who served in the Far East in the Royal Marines and Tom Smith, who served in North Afria, Sicily and Italy with the 5th Battalion Northamptonshire Regiment.

1995 Bob Hadnett performed the opening ceremony of the VE Day Anniversary celebrations at the primary school entrance. Also in the photograph are his wife, Florence (sitting) and behind her, Olive Barrett. Bob was a veteran of the Second World War and saw action with the Royal Corps of Signals in France including the evacuation from Dunkirk in 1940. He was awarded the Military Medal for bravery.

After the war a branch of the Royal British Legion was set up in Spratton and Bob ran the Poppy Appeal from the 1950s, when he came to the village, until 1991.

1995 The Northampton Scouts Band marching along School Road to the opening ceremony of the VE Day 50th Anniversary celebrations in 1995.

1995 The W I Hall decked out with flags and bunting for the VE Day 50th Anniversary celebrations. Traditional home baked teas were served here all afternoon. A barbeque was held and Chris Saul's 1940's sausage recipe sold very well! The day was rounded off with a 1940s disco, community singing and a fish and chip supper.

Friends of St Andrew's Church

The Friends of St Andrew's Church was established in February 1995 to preserve and maintain the fabric of the church and its contents. Since then the Friends have raised approximately £50,000 and used it to repair the rainwater disposal system, restore the stonework to all the windows, renovate the porch, treat the roof timbers and reglaze the windows. In 2003 the Friends undertook a major churchyard survey involving wild flowers and lichen as well as the repair of the churchyard cross and two Grade II listed tombs. A booklet about the churchyard survey was sent to every household in the village. In 2004 funds are being raised to improve the church heating.

The Friends have raised considerable amounts towards all this work from outside charities including the lottery, but also from donations from within the village. The committee has worked hard to organise fund-raising social evenings with speakers and a supper, a casino evening (1997), a Burns Night Supper (2001) two Gilbert and Sullivan evenings (2001 and 2004), a mediaeval banquet (2002) and a weekend of activities including a play, exhibition and flower festival (2004). They were also responsible for installing a plaque by the font to George Washington's great-great grandmother, who was baptised in Spratton Church in 1602.

1996 *Jean Troop baked a christening cake to commemorate the baptism of Amphillis Twigden, great-great grandmother of George Washington in Spratton church in 1602 (See page 40).*

May 2004 *As part of the Churchyard Survey a specially commissioned play about Sir John Swinford and the building of the churchyard cross was performed in church. Seventeen villagers of all ages took part.*

The cast from left to right. Back row: Nigel Townsend (Master Builder), Bill Blowfield (Father John Martin), Darren Sibley (Young Sir John Swinford), Cherill Hammond (Tourist), Tracey Coldwell (Lady Joan Swinford), Sam Hammond (Tourist), Rev Brian Lee (Ghost of Sir John Swinford), Sue Laste(Lady in Waiting), Daniel Mattin (Roger Chambers), Ellie Tee (Elizabeth), Jean Sutch (Lady in Waiting), Diana Wright (Lady in Waiting) Roger Scanlan (Walter Bolekek). Front row: Enid Jarvis (Parishioner), Louise Fletcher (Ralph, an apprentice), Millie Tee (Tourist), Anna Smith (William, an apprentice), Gemma Tee (Tourist), Amy Hewitt (Lady in Waiting), Joan Shaw (Goody Chambers), Adam Snedker (Adam, a tourist). Inset: Sarah Bradnam who made the costumes.

January 2003 History Society Exhibition

The society's first major exhibition was opened by Sarah Bridges, Northamptonshire County Archivist. She was presented with a bouquet by committee member, Pat Greenwood. Left to right: Sarah Bridges, Pat Greenwood, Enid Jarvis, Barry Frenchman, Michael Heaton.

Spratton Local History Society

The society was founded in 1999 with the aim of bringing together people living in Spratton with an interest in local history. Members were encouraged to research historical information which was then copied and archived, and meetings, talks, events and exhibitions were held to promote a wider understanding of the history of the village and the surrounding area.

A family database was set up recording the details of those who lived in the village in the 19th century. Research on individual houses was begun and tape recordings were made of the memories of elderly people about Spratton earlier in the 20th century. The history of the church and churchyard was collected together. Most importantly, a village archive was set up using specialist software for improving and 'repairing' original, often damaged, photographs. In order to achieve this the society was granted an Awards for All Lottery grant.

The society put on its first major exhibition in January 2003 in the Church of England Primary School. It was opened by the County Archivist, Sarah Bridges, and was a great success. There was enormous interest in the displayed photographs and also a flow of new information and pictures that still goes on. The Society has received a Local Heritage Initiative grant to produce this book about the history of Spratton.

Membership of the society has grown from the 15 original members to around 70 in 2004. Four speaker evenings are held over the winter months and guided tours round the village are given to other local history groups and visitors from overseas. The society also provides speakers to give illustrated talks on the history of Spratton.

The Reading Room

Many old maps of Spratton from the early 1900s show a Reading Room marked at the junction of Church Road and Holdenby Road, just along The Walk. This was opened by Mr Smith, the schoolmaster (from 1889 to 1924), in his house by the fields. He held a night school, or evening classes, for anyone in the village who wished to further their knowledge. After Mr Smith's death, the Reading Room was moved to a house opposite the Manor House in School Road.

January 2003 *Members of Spratton Local History Society at the members' preview of the exhibition. All the photographs were prepared and presented in computerised form by Michael Heaton, the society's archivist. The display stands were bought with an Awards For All grant. Left to right: Davina Day, Sue Laste, Jean Sutch, Sue Edwards, Frances Roseblade.*

Chapter Fourteen

SPORT

Spratton Football Club

The year of formation is unknown at present but Spratton Football Club was certainly in existence in 1893. An issue of The Parish Journal of that year included a report of a meeting which took place between the football and cricket clubs. Jack Balderson in an interview in 1963 recounted playing for a well established club from 1894 to 1902 and it would seem that games were played regularly against teams from as far away as Bugbrooke up to the outbreak of World War One

The main requirement for being considered for selection in the early days was that you owned a set of playing kit. Such kits were sold on as players retired from the team. William Manning, who also played in the 1890s, said that he only got the chance of playing when he bought a full kit from someone who was emigrating!

Competition became more formalised in 1896 when

the Club affiliated to The Northamptonshire Football Association which had been established in 1886.

Between the wars the Club competed in the Mid Northants Village League from its formation in 1920 and came out winners in the first two seasons. Further successes as league champions came in 1929-30, 1930-31, 1934-35 and 1936-37 and as League Cup winners in 1936-37 and 1938.

After the end of the Second World War in 1945 local football struggled to get off the ground with the Mid Northants League and its rival, the Central Village League, competing for teams in a relatively small area. Eventually with both leagues on the point of folding, a merger took place in 1953 with a total of 16 clubs, including Spratton, competing in the first season. The new league was named The Central Northants Combination. It is now the Travis Perkins Northamptonshire Combination with 70 clubs fielding a total of 108 teams in the 2003 –2004 season.

Spratton Football Team about 1900
This is one of the oldest photographs in the History Society's archive and unfortunately the names of all the players are not known.
Those named are: Back row: George Voss, ? , Arthur Balderson, Henry Buckby, ?, ?. Middle row: ? , ? , ? , Mr Pateman, Mr Fountain.
Front row: ? , ? , ?

Travel

Up until the 1920s, horse and cart was the usual form of transport to away venues although the team had to walk to the nearer locations. As motorised vehicles began to appear local traders who possessed such equipment were coerced into providing transport. When ownership of bicycles became more common these were frequently used until the beginning of the Second World War. After the war, trucks and vans were mainly used but for a period coaches were hired – Knights Coaches of Old being the usual company until cost became too great and use of private cars became the norm. This is the case up until the present day.

Facilities

From the earliest times a local public house was the headquarters of most village football clubs. In the case of Spratton it was *The Kings Head*, where meetings were held and players changed into playing kit. Washing facilities usually consisted of a couple of buckets of water – hot if you were lucky. For a short period the club used the premises of Spratton and Teeton Conservative Club. The absence of facilities on the field sometimes meant a considerable trek to reach the field. For instance, Spratton at one time or another played in a field below Brixworth Road cemetery and in the field where Golby's Nursery is located. In both cases this was quite a walk from *The Kings Head*. The alternative was to strip out on the field which was not uncommon and sometimes attracted groups of young, and perhaps, no doubt, older women to witness players changing.

Such a situation continued until the late 1960s and into the 70s. Spratton Football Club was the first club in the area to provide changing room and shower facilities on the field when it purchased a wooden building in Leeds, transported it and erected it in 1968 on what is now part of the car park of the recreation field. The Recreation Field Management Committee erected a brick built toilet block. These facilities remained in use until the present dressing room complex was completed in 1989.

In 1977 it became known that a wooden ward on the redundant Welford Road hospital site in Kingsthorpe was available. In conjunction with the Recreation Field Management Committee this was purchased, dismantled and transported to the Recreation Field.

The project in mind was to convert it into a village hall sited on the Recreation Field.

The demise of the committee and a general lack of interest meant that the building sections lay dormant for several years until finally the football club took responsibility to get the project moving again. Fund raising and assistance from the Parish Council resulted in the building being completed in 1983. A public meeting was held in *The Kings Head* to form a committee to set up a social club.

The elected committee soon brought the club into operation which enabled it to welcome players after football matches. This arrangement was unique as far as village clubs were concerned and served as a fore-runner for what is now regarded as a standard requirement for acceptance into the higher divisions of most football leagues.

Dick Spearman

Football Team Honours since 1953

First Team

Premier Division League Winners - 1985 and 1987

Premier Division League Runners Up - 1978, 1979, 1986

Premier KO Cup Winners - 1978,1985, 1986, 2000

Premier KO Cup Runners Up - 1972, 1974, 1987, 1988 and 1995

Division One League Winners - 1957, 1958, 1959, 1963, 1976 and 1994

Division One League Runners Up - 1961, 1962

Division KO Cup Winners - 1957, 1965, 1993

Division KO Runners Up - 1961, 1963

Mid Northants Village League Winners 1920-1921

Back row from left to right: Victor Bell, ?. Standing: 'Captain' Taylor, B Taylor, Ebenezer Copson, M Hayter, Fred Archer, Archibald Copson, Walt Archer, B Snegnel, Thomas Wykes. Sitting: Joseph Copson, Arthur Wood (landlord of the King's Head), Arthur Horne, Mr Thorley (the baker), P Battams. Front row: A Harrison, S Page (the butcher).

Mid Northants Village League Winners 1929-1930

Back row from left to right: Jaby Eames, Leslie Green, 'Nebby' Cattell, Bill Berridge. Third row: Micky Cook, Bill Byrne, 'Shotty' Horne, John Tarrant, Fred Archer, Joe Balderson. Second row: Horace Hillery, Hector Wykes, 'Chub' Eldred, Walter Churchill, George Hider, Dick Manning, Tommy Harris. Front row: Fred Buckby, Luke Taylor, Percy Cook, Walter Crane.

1936 Football Team Village League and Cup winners (the 'double')

Back row. Left to right: Archibald Squires (Treasurer), Fred Pateman, W Rendall, Cyril Emery, Jim Griffin, George Pateman (Vice Captain), Bill Byrne, Frank Smith, Bill (Nebby) Cattell, Joe Balderson.

Front row: Joe Billing (Secretary), Luke Taylor, Cecil Stowe, Frank Copson (Captain), Charles (Tunk) Copson, Percy Cook.

Sitting on ground: Phil Emery, Tom Cooper.

1957 Northamptonshire Combination Division 1: League and Knockout Cup 'double' winners

Back row from left to right: Jack Walmsley, Bill Pateman, Tony Dunkley, Bob Tite, Roy Mason, Elwyn Morgan, Ken Jarvis, William Cattell , Malcolm Wykes, John Eldred, George Eldred, Alan Wykes.

Front row: Tony Wykes, 'Grandy' Gradd (from Switzerland), Peter Churchill, Keith Valentine, Percy Pateman, Pop Coleman.

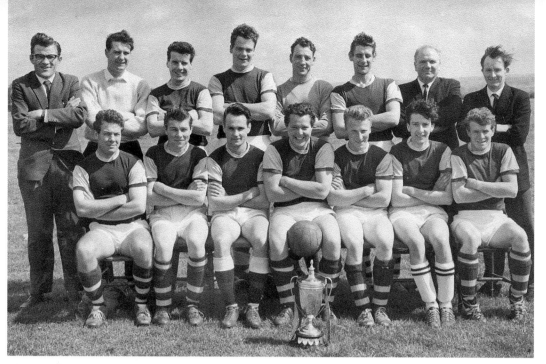

1964 - 1965 Northamptonshire Combination Division 1 – Knockout cup winners
Back row from left to right: Jeff Tite, Terry Hardwick, George Costello, Bob Bartlett, Ken Martin, Tom Horne, Bert Buckby, Ted Wilkes.
Front row: Roy Mason, Brian Billingham, Harry Thomas, Joe Hayter, John Wykes, Brian Savage, Graham Billingham.

c1968 Football team
Back row from left to right: John (Ginger) Wykes, Freddy Hollowell, Tom Horne, Neil Tarrant, Edward Barrett, Ted Messinger .
Front row: Brian Billingham, Jeff Buckby, Harry Thomas, Steven Harris, Terry Mould.

Boxing

Jeff Tite

Born in 1926, Jeff was working in farming during the war. He suffered a serious accident on the farm and took a year to recover and convalesce. After the war he married Jean Buckby from Spratton and came to live with her parents for a few months before buying Yew Tree Cottage, one of the cottages that stood on the site of the present Millennium Rose Garden. It was a thatched cottage with an outside toilet on the other side of the road – the main danger in crossing was from a herd of cows going down the road!

Jeff met his good friend, Roy Davies who had started boxing a few years before, and was determined that Spratton Youth Club would get their revenge over Brixworth Youth Club 'in the ring'. Roy asked Jeff to spar with him and realised at once that he was a natural fighter. Jeff had his first fight on September 15th 1947. In all he had 85 welter-weight and middleweight contests over five years, and he won 67 of these.

After he retired, Jeff was publican of *The Kings Head* for three years from 1st December 1953, taking over from Fred Turnell.

1948 *Jeff Tite from Spratton at the start of his boxing career.*

Motor Cycle Racing

Maria Costello

Freelance journalist, Maria Costello from Spratton has had a most successful career on the motor cycling race tracks recently. She has become the fastest woman motor cyclist at the Manx Grand Prix on the Isle of Man with a record breaking lap of 114.7 mph. She was riding a Padgett's Suzuki GSXR 600 RR. In 2004 just seven men beat her in the Senior race at the Isle of Man TT where she celebrated taking 8th place and a Silver Replica Award. She was riding an Island Motorcycles Ltd Honda CBR 600 RR.

She also won the Manx Motorcycle Club's trophy for the female making the most meritorious performance of the two week event.

2004 *Maria Costello riding her Honda 600 at the Isle of Man TT race in 2004.*

Spratton Cricket Club

Before the Second World War, the cricket club used to play in a field on Hall Lane on Gilby's farm. This field, however, was ploughed up during the war and, with men away in the Services, cricket activities were suspended.

The team was re-formed in 1945 by Jim Griffin, who became captain, and Tom Puttnam, who became secretary. Reg Tarrant took over the finances as treasurer. The only grass field available was on Mr Morgan's sheep farm at Miller's Barn (Grange Farm). On Saturday mornings on his way home from work, Jim Griffin would get the bus conductor to stop and let him off at Miller's Barn. He then cut and marked out the wicket, walked home, changed and then cycled back to play in the match. Tom Puttnam used to ferry some of the team to matches in his fish van and Peter Churchill remembers the smell well!

In 1947 the Cricket Club managed to find a field nearer to the village on Tommy Wykes' farm near Broomhill. He was nicknamed 'Spinner' for obvious reasons! During the post war period the team played in the Mid Northants Village League and was considerably strengthened by the young men returning from the war and especially by two players, Dennis Smith and Alfred Horne. Den Smith, who had married a Spratton girl, came from Brixworth and became captain. Alf Horne was a Spratton lad who played professional football for Northampton Town, Watford and Corby. He finished his career with Spratton!

In 1950 the club moved to one of Dick Darling's fields below the old cemetery and ceased playing league cricket. The highlights of the so-called 'friendly' matches were those against Creaton. Not only was there great rivalry between the teams, but also between the two captains, Dick Darling and Eric Pember. They were both farmers and good friends off the field, but deadly rivals on it.

After one more move, this time to the Recreation Ground, the Cricket Club was disbanded in 1955. Key players such as Dick Darling and Bill McColl had moved away from the village as had a number of younger team members.

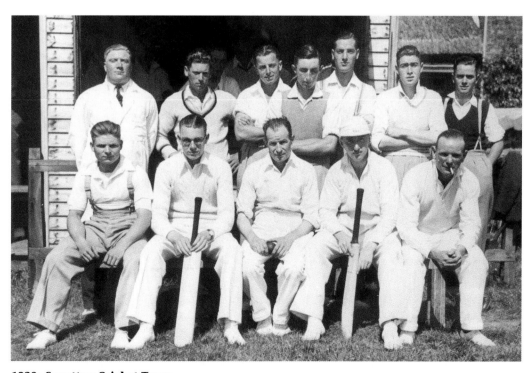

1930s Spratton Cricket Team
Back row from left to right: Bill Leeson, Bill Sharp, Jack Riddle, 'Peggy' Martin, Tom Buckby, Les Crane, Ron Bounds.
Front row: Tom Cooper, Jack Austin, George Wogan, Bob Wykes, Joe Billing.

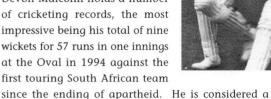

Vallance Jupp (1891 – 1960)

Vallance Jupp was a great help to Spratton Cricket Club in getting started again after the Second World War. He had been an outstanding County and England Test cricketer during the 1920s and 1930s, playing for England from 1921 – 1928. He played for Sussex 1909 – 1922, Marylebone Cricket Club 1923 – 1933 and Northamptonshire 1923 – 1938. He captained Northamptonshire from 1927 – 1931 and was Wisden Cricketer of the Year in 1928.

When he retired from cricket he settled in Yew Tree Lane in Spratton and opened a sports shop in St Giles' Street, Northampton. He donated equipment and much time and enthusiasm to Spratton Cricket Club. His stepson, Bill McColl, was fine amateur cricketer and played for several years for Spratton.

Charles T Studd (1860 – 1931)

Charles Thomas Studd was born in Spratton in December 1860. His parents were Edward Studd, a weathy retired planter and Dorothy, who at the time were living at Spratton Hill House. He was one of six brothers who, together with a half-brother, all played first class cricket. Charles Thomas ('C.T.') and his brother George also played for England. The family moved from Spratton when Charles was still a boy.

By the age of 21 his career was described as 'one long blaze of cricketing glory'; he had scored 1,249 runs for Cambridge University and the MCC, including a century against the Australians. His record of 128 wickets, together with the number of runs, exceeds that of the famous W G Grace. In addition he toured Australia with the Hon Ivo Bligh to bring back the original Ashes for England.

Charles died at a mission station in the Belgian Congo in 1931 at the age of 70. He had given away his inheritance and spent the years since 1885 as a missionary in China, India and Africa. 'Spratton' Studd is immortalised by the poet John Masefield as 'Cambridge Studd, the bright bat debonair.'

Devon Malcolm

The distinguished cricketer Devon Malcolm (born 1963 in Kingston, Jamaica) now lives in Spratton. He was a right-arm fast bowler and took 128 wickets playing for England in Test matches from 1989 – 1997. He has played county cricket for Derbyshire from 1984 – 1997, Northamptonshire from 1998 – 2000 and Leicestershire 2001 – 2003, and was Wisden Cricketer of the Year in 1995.

1920s *Vallance Jupp (left) walking out to open the innings for Northampton with Frank E Wooley. The old Northampton Stand can be seen in the background.*

Devon Malcolm holds a number of cricketing records, the most impressive being his total of nine wickets for 57 runs in one innings at the Oval in 1994 against the first touring South African team since the ending of apartheid. He is considered a 'quick' bowler, which is faster than 'fast', and this is a record for a quick bowler and also the sixth best bowling figure in the history of cricket.

He has helped with distributing cricket gear around the South African townships including Soweto and has often met Nelson Mandela.

1990s *Devon Malcolm, who lives in Spratton, bowling for England in a one day international against New Zealand. He was 'Man of the Match' for his performance.*

Rugby

Matt Dawson

Matt Dawson of Northampton Saints and England lived in Spratton for a short time and was a teacher at Spratton Hall School. He is the most capped England scrum half ever with 51 caps and was, of course, part of the winning World Cup team in Australia 2003. He captained the England team in their victorious Six Nations Championship in 2000 and regularly appears in the media, writing newspaper articles or expressing his opinions on TV.

Ben Cohen

Ben Cohen of Northampton Saints and England was born in Northampton in September 1978, went to school in Kingsthorpe and now lives in Spratton. He has played over 100 games for Northampton Saints, having begun his career with them when he was 17 years old.

Ben counts as the highlights of his career: winning the European Cup with Northampton in 2000; his first try for England in the same year; all of the autumn internationals in 2002 and, last but definitely not least, England's World Cup success in Australia in 2003.

2003 *Ben Cohen (left) holds aloft the coveted Webb Ellis Trophy with team member Jason Robinson in Sydney in 2003. England had just beaten Australia 20—17 in the Rugby World Cup Final.*

INDEX OF NAMES

1930s *Hector Wykes (second from left) ran a Salvage Company with this van. William Leeson stands on the right.*